THE SOUTH AFRICAN
NATIVES

THE SOUTH AFRICAN NATIVES

THEIR PROGRESS AND PRESENT CONDITION

EDITED BY

THE SOUTH AFRICAN NATIVE RACES COMMITTEE

A SUPPLEMENT TO "THE NATIVES OF SOUTH AFRICA:
THEIR ECONOMIC AND SOCIAL CONDITION"

NEGRO UNIVERSITIES PRESS
NEW YORK

Originally published in 1908
by John Murray

Reprinted 1969 by
Negro Universities Press
A DIVISION OF GREENWOOD PUBLISHING CORP.
NEW YORK

SBN 8371-1539-6

PRINTED IN UNITED STATES OF AMERICA

CONTENTS

CHAPTER IV

CHAPTER V

CHAPTER VI

CHAPTER VII

CHAPTER VIII

THE

SOUTH AFRICAN NATIVE RACES COMMITTEE

MEMBERS OF COMMITTEE

vii

INTRODUCTION

THE purpose and scope of this volume may be stated in a few words. Seven years ago the South African Native Races Committee published the chief results of their inquiries in a book entitled "The Natives of South Africa." Since that time important changes have taken place in native affairs, and others are impending. Much valuable information has become available. The Committee believe, therefore, that the time has come when a supplementary volume, describing the new order of things, dealing concisely with some of the more important developments, and stating some of the chief results of recent investigations, may be useful. They have not attempted to go over the same ground as that of the previous book. The scope of the present volume is more limited. But the Committee hope that something may be gained by concentrating attention on a few features.

The years which have passed since the signing of the Peace of Vereeniging have brought many changes of importance in native affairs, and some of the changes are for the better. A new spirit of progress is abroad. The natives begin to do something for their own improvement. They value education more than they did. They have opened schools. They have established churches. They have their own newspapers and their own political organisations. Along with healthy, though sometimes misdirected, activity is a growing power of initiative—a source of anxiety at present but of promise for the future. On the whole, too, there is a more sympathetic feeling among the whites. Societies for the study of native questions have been formed on much the same lines as this Committee. The futility of a barren policy of repression is recognised. The South African colonies begin to face the native problem with a new sense of its importance, its interest, and its possibilities. The labours of the Inter-Colonial Commission on Native Affairs of 1903–5 and the Natal Commission of 1906–7 have resulted in the collection of a mass of information and in suggestions which claim the immediate attention of the Colonial Governments. The work of those Commissions is already beginning to bear fruit. Questions are approached with a more open mind. Increased support is being given to native education, and in various ways the position of the natives has been improved.

Not the least significant of the recent developments is the joint action which has been taken by the Colonial Governments in investigating matters affecting the natives. The possibility of a South African Native policy is at length beginning to emerge from conflicting methods and theories. Grave differences of opinion still exist, but the colonies have at least united in investigating the question. The reports of the Commissions have provided a basis for a uniform and progressive system of administration, and the urgent need of agreement with regard to it will no doubt lead, and possibly more rapidly than many imagine, to the adoption of more harmonious systems of administration. Divergencies of local conditions will no doubt necessitate different administrative methods. But agreement on the general principles of native policy no longer seems outside the range of practical politics.

In the following pages the Committee have endeavoured

to trace the remarkable economic and social changes among the natives, the progress of education among them, the growth of the native churches, and recent developments in regard to taxation and the holding of land. They are also glad to include in this volume a chapter on the administration of natives in the various colonies by Sir Godfrey Lagden, whose work as Resident Commissioner of Basutoland, Commissioner of Native Affairs in the Transvaal, and Chairman of the Inter-Colonial Commission will be familiar to all students of the native question.

The Committee have endeavoured to discuss the questions considered in this volume with appreciation of their difficulty, in the light of facts, and in no censorious spirit. They recognise the grave responsibility of the white colonists of South Africa in administering the affairs of a large and increasing population of natives living under widely differing conditions and fast acquiring new ideas and ambitions. They are aware that the native question presents problems which can only be gradually solved by local knowledge and experience. But they trust that their efforts to collect information and to submit suggestions may be of some assistance in removing misapprehensions and promoting right views. Many past efforts on the part of a white population to deal with problems elsewhere akin to those which now lie before South Africa have been more or less failures. The hope of those who have prepared this book is that it may be otherwise in that country, if only there is a desire to be just and patient and to remember the responsibilities attaching to the possession of power.

The Committee welcome the establishment in Johannesburg and Durban of societies with like objects to their own. They believe that there is ample room for the work of such societies and others.

The Committee desire to record their thanks to their correspondents in South Africa and others to whom they are indebted for much valuable information and advice. As in the case of the former book, the preparation of this volume has devolved upon a small Executive Committee, and other members of so large a General Committee cannot be held responsible for particular statements and conclusions.

THE SOUTH AFRICAN NATIVES

CHAPTER I

OCCUPATIONS OF NATIVES: THE LABOUR QUESTION

§ 1. NATIVE OCCUPATIONS

BEFORE the rule of the white man was firmly established, the life of the natives alternated between fierce intertribal conflicts and the hardly less demoralising stagnation into which they sank in times of peace. Among military peoples such as the Zulus and Matabele the men were mainly engaged in the pursuits of war and the chase. The virtues of courage and obedience were inculcated by a training of merciless severity, the fruits of which may be seen to-day in the splendid physique and fine manners of these natives, often combined with lack of mental energy and contempt for manual labour. When not engaged in war or hunting, all tribal natives found their chief occupations in tending their flocks and herds and raising crops of maize or mealies and Kafir corn. Much of the agricultural work was, and is still, left to the women, who hoe and weed the fields, reap and gather in the harvest—sometimes with, sometimes without, the help of the men—strip the mealies from the cob, and thresh, winnow and grind the grain. The women also make the native beer from Kafir corn, carry the water and firewood, and do the cooking. The men milk the cows

I

and sometimes work in the fields ; the older boys look after the goats and cattle, and the smaller boys and girls scare the birds from the crops. This division of work varies somewhat in the different districts. In Mashonaland the men cultivate their fields side by side with their wives, and, in the summer at any rate, take a fair share of the work. But, as a general rule, the men seem to have an easier life in the kraals than the women, although their indolence has frequently been exaggerated. Both the men and women have often considerable manual dexterity. They construct their huts with skill. They make wooden pitchers, dishes and milk-pails and simple pottery, weave baskets and grass mats, twist wire bangles, make string from rushes or bark, and are fond of bead-work and wood-carving. In the days when iron implements could not easily be bought from the traders they are said to have produced fair iron-work, and they still manufacture some rough metal utensils. But their progress in industrial pursuits has been insignificant. Apart from European training, they have developed no form of trade or commerce.[1]

Such, stated briefly, were the ordinary occupations of the natives before the white man's demand for labour set them moving over the country to new and sometimes uncongenial employments. In their tribal society they seemed to have reached a stage at which incentives to progress failed them. They lived under easy climatic conditions ; their wants were few ; and the communal policy and rigid custom of tribal life gave individual tribesmen little opportunity or inducement to improve their lot. To make any further advance they needed the stimulus which contact with more progressive communities could alone supply.

To the natives have now come the fruits of the present era of peace and comparative prosperity. Devastating

---

[1] Much information with regard to the kraal life of the natives may be found in Mr. Dudley Kidd's " The Essential Kafir."

hordes no longer sweep over the country. White magistrates secure the tribesmen from the tyranny of a Tshaka
or a Dingan; and most of the natives are now practically
disarmed. But the cessation of tribal strife was an artificial,
not an organic, change. It was not the result of a growing
spirit of industry, but an incident of white administration.
It found the natives unprepared to take advantage of the
new conditions. The respect for law and authority which
they had acquired in their tribal life enabled competent
administrators to guide them successfully into the ways of
peace and good order. The spirit of industry had still to
be developed. The men continued to look with contempt
on manual labour, which during generations of warfare had
been left almost exclusively to the women, and their scanty
needs supplied no effective incentives to progress. Hence
the establishment of intertribal peace made for a time a
perilous breach in native life. In many districts the men
were content to subsist in idleness on the toil of their wives
and daughters. Demoralised by indolence, the natives of
South Africa might easily have gone the way of other
native peoples whose vigour has been sapped by contact
with civilisation. Two things have saved them from this
fate—the influence and teaching of the missionaries, and
the almost insatiable demand of the white colonists for unskilled labour. The missionaries have raised the standard
of native life; the white employers have supplied strong
inducements to industry. And this demand for labour has
not only given the natives the opportunity of satisfying
new needs which the spread of Christianity and education
has evoked; it has itself been a most effectual educational
agency. It has brought the natives into touch with the
white communities. If it has exposed them to the vices of
civilisation, it has also done much to stimulate among them
a new and healthy spirit of progress. Operating upon
primitive instincts, economic forces are singularly far-

reaching in their effects. While building up their own fortunes, white employers have set moving a series of changes in the conditions of native life destined to have a decisive bearing on the future history of South Africa. The tenacity with which the natives cling to their tribal life prevents these changes taking place with alarming rapidity. However slowly they may be accomplished, they are the first symptoms of a veritable social revolution. Natives cannot come into contact with the freedom of civilised life, enter into individual contracts and secure earnings formerly undreamt of, and yet retain their old communal ideas and submit to the caprice and exactions of their tribal superiors. Slowly but surely the economic changes must undermine the tribal societies, already weakened by the spread of education and by the growing influence of the white magistrate.

Partly from racial feeling, partly from force of circumstances, the whites in South Africa rely almost exclusively on the natives for unskilled labour. Whether wise or not, this policy has made the question of native labour a matter of vital importance to all the white communities. There is indeed a distinct danger of its being regarded too exclusively as the determining factor with regard to native policy. The education of natives, the amount and incidence of their taxes, their rights with regard to the occupation and tenure of land, and other matters, are too often considered less on their general merits than in reference to their bearing on the supply of native labour. This tendency accounts for many mistakes as to native affairs. Its existence makes a thorough understanding of the labour problem essential to a right appreciation of the views generally held in South Africa with regard to native policy.

On the whole, the demands of the whites for native labour have been met with remarkable readiness. A large proportion of the male natives now enter the service of

white employers. Nevertheless, the tribal natives still
cling with an intense attachment to their life on the tribal
lands. Even when they are attracted by high wages to
the industrial centres, they generally stay only for a few
months at a time, and return to their kraals as soon as
they have completed their contracts. Thus the Kafir who
works on the Rand seldom becomes a genuine miner. In
almost all cases. he is an agriculturist or herdsman
temporarily working in a mine in order to obtain the
money he needs for the purchase of cattle or for some
other purpose connected with his tribal life. Upon this
system of migratory labour most of the industries of South
Africa depend. With the exception of the farmers who
provide accommodation and land for their employees
and their families, the whites in South Africa rely on
the migrant native for practically all purposes involving
manual labour. The system no doubt has its serious
disadvantages. Natives continually leave their employment just when they are becoming efficient. A good
harvest often makes them reluctant to seek work, and
the cost and difficulty of organising this fluctuating supply
of labour are a source of constant anxiety. But incon-
venient and uneconomical as the system is, it has many
advantages for employers. It provides them with a vast
supply of cheap labour ; it burdens them with no pauper
class ; it gives rise to no labour organisations ; it leaves
unskilled labour with little or no representation in South
African politics. Its greatest recommendation is that it
preserves the tribal and family life of the natives, and to
some extent avoids the evils which invariably arise when
uneducated tribal natives are allowed to live in the towns.
Tribal discipline and tribal sentiment supply the only
moral restraints that as yet have any effective hold on this
class of natives, who are unfitted for the unguarded
freedom of civilised life. Unless effectual precautions are

taken to keep them apart from the white population, and to prevent them obtaining intoxicating liquors, even their short visits to industrial centres too often result in their returning to their kraals contaminated by the vices of the towns. It is true that these dangers are at length being recognised, and steps are being taken by municipalities and employers to place the natives employed in the towns in separate locations under competent supervision. But whatever precautions may be taken, it is undesirable to induce the natives to abandon their tribal life prematurely ; and for the present the system of temporary employment is a necessity.

In most parts of South Africa the labourers are usually natives of Bantu stock, but in the west of Cape Colony, where the Bantus are not numerous, much of the labour is supplied by Hottentots and "coloured" people of mixed races. The Hottentots, of whom there are about 86,000 in the Colony, are generally in the service of white employers, often as domestic servants or farm labourers. The coloured people, who number about 300,000, form a large proportion of the population in most of the western districts. Many of them are working on the farms, roads, railways and docks, and as domestic servants, assistants in stores and laundries, clerks, drivers, masons, carpenters, painters and labourers, and in many other occupations. They seem to be less closely attached to the land than the pure Bantu natives, and a much larger proportion of them are engaged in commercial and industrial employments. In the other colonies they are far fewer, but as they are generally more progressive than the ordinary natives, they are often useful members of the community.[1]

---

[1] A large amount of labour is also supplied by Indians, Chinese, and the so-called "Malays," but these immigrants do not come within the scope of the present volume.

TABLE A

POPULATION OF BRITISH SOUTH AFRICA

(As Shown in Census of 1904.)

	Area Sq. Miles.	European or White.	Bantu.	Mixed and other Coloured Races.	Total.
Cape Colony . .	276,995	579,741	1,424,787[1]	405,276[2]	2,409,804
Natal	35,371	97,109	904,041	107,604[3]	1,108,754
Transvaal . . ⎫	111,196	297,277[4]	937,127[5]	35,547[6]	1,269,951
Swaziland . . ⎭	6,536	890	84,529	72	85,491
Orange River Colony .	50,392	142,679	229,149	15,487[7]	387,315
Southern Rhodesia (Mashonaland and Matabeleland) . . .	143,830	12,623	591,197[8]	1,944[9]	605,764
Basutoland . . .	10,293	895	347,731	222	348,848
Bechuanaland Protectorate . . .	275,000	1,004	119,411 (about)	361	120,776
Total . .	909,613	1,132,218	4,637,972	566,513	6,336,703

[1] Includes Fingos, 310,720 ; and Kafirs and Bechuanas, 1,114,067.

[2] Includes Hottentots, 85,892 ; Namaquas, 62 ; Bushmen, 4,168 ; Korannas, 1,138 ; Griquas, 6,289 ; Mixed, 279,662 ; Malays, 15,682 ; Indians, 8,489 ; Mozambiques, 1,433 ; Chinese, 1,380 ; and others, 1,081.

[3] Includes Hottentots, 100 ; Griquas, 983 ; Mixed, 3,160 ; Indians and other Asiatics, 100,918 ; Mauritians, 1,232 ; St. Helena, 1,150 ; and others, 61.

[4] Includes military forces.

[5] Includes 144,231 Portuguese and East Coast natives, many of whom were only temporary residents.

[6] Includes Cape and Bastard, 10,077 ; Mixed and Other Coloured, 12,965 ; Indians, 9,979 ; non-British Asiatics, 1,411 ; Malays, 904 ; and other Asiatics (British subjects), 201.

[7] Includes Hottentots, 2,785 ; Griquas, 683 ; Mozambiques, 242 ; Other Mixed, 11,481 ; Asiatics, 253 ; and Other Coloured, 43.

[8] Includes 6,991 natives from outside British South Africa.

[9] Includes Asiatics and Other Coloured persons.

7

An analysis of the census statistics of 1904 (which have been summarised in the annexed Table B) reveals three noteworthy facts :

(i) the smallness of the class of dependents, (ii) the predominance of agriculture as a native occupation, and (iii) the wide range of industrial, commercial and professional employments in which natives are engaged.

The smallness of the dependent class, composed mainly of children at school or not engaged in some specified employment, is to some extent accounted for by the early age at which native children begin to work. But it also shows that the majority of the adult natives, though often reluctant to engage in hard continuous labour, rank, nevertheless, in the bread-winning classes. The predominance of agriculture is even greater than it appears from the figures in the annexed table, for a large proportion of the natives who were returned as engaged in commercial or industrial pursuits were primarily agriculturists, and were only temporarily engaged in other occupations. The elaborate tables of occupations compiled by the census officials in Cape Colony, the Transvaal and the Orange River Colony, show that large numbers of natives are employed in many capacities in industrial, and, to a lesser extent, in commercial employments, and that their positions demand very different degrees of responsibility and skill. By far the larger proportion of these natives, it is true, fail to rise above the lower grades of work. Most of them are simply unskilled manual labourers, but an increasing number are finding their way into skilled employments. Their competition in various trades is already regarded with anxiety by the white artisans. Some thousands have been trained by the missionaries as ministers, evangelists and teachers ; but, as a rule, there is little opening for them in the higher professions. Apparently at present only exceptional natives are capable of qualifying themselves for such

TABLE B

OCCUPATIONS OF NATIVES AND OTHER COLOURED PEOPLE

MALES

CLASS OF OCCUPATION.	CAPE COLONY.		NATAL.		TRANSVAAL AND SWAZILAND.		ORANGE RIVER COLONY		TOTAL.	
	Natives.	Other Coloured.	Natives.	Other Coloured.	Natives.	Other Coloured.	Natives.	Other Coloured.	Natives.	Other Coloured.
Professional . .	3,670	819	1,702	472	2,167	151	562	32	8,101	1,474
Domestic . .	5,229	7,333	30,049	3,911	23,629	3,522	6,239	682	65,146	15,448
Commercial & Industrial	67,945	61,997	20,369	18,770	131,028	12,655	11,629	1,213	230,971	94,635
Agricultural . .	389,597	61,829	211,446¹	26,698	175,172	3,706	60,173	3,464	836,388	95,697
Dependents (²) .	225,024	74,445	163,200	16,985	198,838	4,184	28,204	2,213	615,266	97,827
Indefinite & Unspecified	1,263	1,245	—	271	5,736	426	13,257	856	20,256	2,798
Total Males .	692,728	207,668	426,766	67,107	536,570	24,644	120,064	8,460	1,776,128	307,879

FEMALES

CLASS OF OCCUPATION.	CAPE COLONY.		NATAL.		TRANSVAAL AND SWAZILAND.		ORANGE RIVER COLONY		TOTAL.	
	Natives.	Other Coloured.	Natives.	Other Coloured.	Natives.	Other Coloured.	Natives.	Other Coloured.	Natives.	Other Coloured.
Professional . .	995	625	—	45	26	25	31	8	1,052	703
Domestic . .	61,568	105,321	10,232	19,518	18,092	5,128	32,642	2,784	122,534	132,751
Commercial & Industrial	1,007	2,187	—	309	15	179	1,230	209	2,252	2,884
Agricultural . .	434,741	12,132	292,501¹	6,088	268,655	1,555	46,253	1,898	1,042,150	21,673
Dependents (²) .	231,751	75,516	174,542	14,460	196,874	3,979	28,150	2,050	631,317	96,005
Indefinite & Unspecified	1,997	1,827	—	77	1,424	109	779	78	4,200	2,091
Total Females .	732,059	197,608	477,275	40,497	485,086	10,975	109,085	7,027	1,803,505	256,107
Total Males & Females	1,424,787	405,276	904,041	107,604	1,021,656	35,619	229,149	15,487	3,579,633	563,986

¹ Includes agricultural, pastoral, mineral and other primary producers.

² Includes 'children not returned as engaged in any of the above classes of occupations.

The above table does not include Southern Rhodesia (except as regards natives in the employment of Europeans in that country) or Basutoland or the Bechuanaland Protectorate, but many labourers from these countries who were temporarily resident in Cape Colony, Natal, the Transvaal and the Orange River Colony are included in the above figures.

In SOUTHERN RHODESIA there were, at the time of the Census, 27,057 natives in the employment of Europeans, engaged in the following occupations :

	MALES.	FEMALES.	TOTAL.
B.S.A. police, constables and gaol warders .	422	—	422
Farm, plot and market garden labourers . .	3,484	20	3,504
Persons engaged in domestic duties . . .	6,743	248	6,991
„ „ on railways . . .	2,483	—	2,483
„ „ about offices, shops and stores	1,054	—	1,054
„ „ working for carpenters, and bricklayers	351	—	351
General labourers and all other undefined outdoor workers	1,213	—	1,213
Woodcutters	759	—	759
Mine workers	10,280	—	10,280
TOTAL	26,789	268	27,057

positions. But the progress which they have made in other directions has already produced a large and important class of natives with requirements and capabilities very different from those of the agricultural tribesman.

In the following pages it is proposed to consider in some detail the changes which these new occupations have caused in the ordinary tribal life of the natives, the conditions of their various employments, and some of the social aspects of the economic revolution which is so quietly but effectually taking place.

(a) Changes in the Occupations of the Kraal Natives

Although in many respects the kraal life of the natives often remains singularly unaltered, the demand for labour has already led to significant changes in their habits and customs. They are still primarily agriculturists or herdsmen working on their own account, but a very large proportion of them have now also become temporary wage-earners. It is a common practice for able-bodied men to leave their homes from time to time to enter the service of white employers. For this purpose they often travel great distances. As a rule they do not remain employed for more than about six months. In this time they can often, without much difficulty, save about £10 or £12 out of their earnings, and with this money they generally return to their kraals and resume their normal occupations. While this practice takes them into many other employments, it has greatly strengthened their position as agriculturists. With the savings which they bring home they are able to make good the ravages of rinderpest among their cattle and to buy the implements which they need for the cultivation of their fields. In many districts large numbers of European ploughs have in this

way been purchased by natives ; and, as ploughing involves
the use of cattle, the introduction of the plough has compelled the men to take a share in the work of the kraal.
But the old wasteful methods of cultivation are still
generally adhered to, manuring is almost unknown, and
even the ploughing is seldom done efficiently. Some of
the more progressive natives are beginning to grow
produce for the market, and in the east of Cape Colony
natives keep flocks of merino sheep and sell the wool for
export ; but most kraal natives only attempt to raise such
crops as they need for their own use. The prevalence of
cattle diseases is a further check on the prosperity of these
natives, whose wealth is mainly invested in their flocks
and herds. But there are many indications that their
possessions are increasing, and that their standard of
living is gradually rising. They are purchasing large
quantities of clothing, blankets and other European goods.[1]
In progressive districts the huts are being improved, and
stone buildings are being erected. Considerable sums
have been contributed by the natives for educational
and religious purposes. The statistics contained in the
census with regard to their agricultural stock also supply
evidence of growing prosperity. To take one instance,
which may be regarded as typical of a progressive tribal
community, the returns for Basutoland, which is practically
a native reserve (with a population of about 350,000),
showed that in 1904 there were 63,677 horses, 209,883
cattle, 14,388 ploughs and 1,320 waggons in the country.
Notwithstanding the inertia of tribal life, there are
significant signs of coming change. The kraal native is

---

[1] A trader in Basutoland informed the Native Affairs Commission of
1903–5 that the Basuto were purchasing blankets, cotton goods, dress
materials (cotton and woollen), hats, boots, shirts, tables, chairs, bed-
steads, lamps, hut doors, sardines, jam, golden syrup, tea, coffee, sugar,
etc.—Qs. 39,478, 39,489, 39,511.

beginning to feel the stimulus of new ideas, and is learning to look after his own interests. Year by year he submits with increasing reluctance to the exactions of his chiefs and headmen, and finds the obligations which tribal custom imposes upon him more irksome and distasteful. And the pressure of population is making it increasingly difficult for young men to live in the old way within the tribal limits. Native methods of cultivation are extremely wasteful, and some of the tribal communities are already outgrowing the land available for their use. It is therefore fast becoming necessary for them to adopt better methods of cultivation or to find new outlets for some of their members.

(b) Farming

The farmer has two considerable advantages over other competitors for native labour. He offers the natives a congenial and healthy form of employment. He can provide them with land, on which they can live with their families in their accustomed manner. These inducements have attracted large numbers of natives to the farms, some as labourers desiring employment, others as labour-tenants in search of a home. Both these classes of natives work for the farmer, but in distinct capacities and on different terms. The labourer or "volunteer," as he is sometimes called, generally stays only for a few months at a time, and remains in the continuous employment of the farmer throughout his period of service. The labour-tenant, on the contrary, lives permanently on the farm, and gives his services when required during a portion of the year as a condition of his tenancy.

Some farmers employ their volunteer labourers by the day ; but the usual practice is to pay a monthly wage and to provide the labourer with food and lodging, and sometimes with a small piece of land for the support of his family. The rate of wage varies greatly in the different districts. In the west of Cape Colony 40s. a month appears to be about the current wage, and some wine-farmers give their labourers 2s. to 3s. and two bottles of wine a day. In parts of the Transvaal where labour is scarce the pay is equally high, and in the Orange River Colony farmers sometimes pay 30s. a month; but these rates are exceptional, and apparently on most South African farms the labourers only receive from 10s. to 20s. a month, in addition to their food and accommodation, or 1s. to 1s. 6d. a day. Some farmers still pay their natives in stock, a practice which seems to be unsatisfactory on both sides; the farmers complaining that their labourers overlook any rise in the value of stock, and the natives sometimes having to accept payment for their services in "measly goats." This system of remuneration is not calculated to improve the relations between the farmers and their employees, and will no doubt have to be abandoned sooner or later for cash payments.

If the farmer takes an intelligent interest in his natives, the position of the farm labourer has many advantages. He is able to live on the land with his family; he is engaged in work for which by his tastes and habits he is well adapted; and his employer often provides him with clothing and medical attendance. Moreover, from a good employer he receives not only protection but a practical training, which is not the least useful form of native education. It is not surprising therefore that a farmer who treats his employees considerately and pays them a reasonable wage seems generally able to obtain the labour he needs, and can sometimes get labourers to stay with him for a number of years. But in far too many cases the farmer takes little interest in the welfare of his natives, and as a class the farm labourers are generally underpaid and miserably housed and fed. " I think," writes Mr. J. Simpson, the

Resident Magistrate at Lusikisiki, in his reply to the queries of the Native Affairs Commission,

> if the farmer could be induced to give his servants, particularly shepherds, more pay and better house accommodation, and a better class of food, the labour difficulty, so far as he is concerned, would disappear. When one considers that a farmer will place in sole charge of a "boy" 1,000 or more sheep, worth perhaps £1,000, and only pay him from 7s. to 15s. per month, and provide him with a house, in many cases not sufficiently decent for a favourite dog, it is not to be expected that the servant will take that interest in his master's property that he would if it were otherwise. . . . It is this want of consideration for the comfort of the native servant that keeps him at his kraal, even if he has to exist on half rations.

It is clear that to some extent the remedy for the alleged scarcity and inefficiency of farm labour lies in the hands of the farmers themselves. Better treatment, fair wages and proper accommodation would, no doubt, go far to solve the labour problem on many South African farms. In justice to the farmer it must be remembered that his position as an employer has its peculiar difficulties. His need of labour is not constant. He generally has to rely on servants who will not work continuously for more than half the year ; and it is impossible for him to offer remuneration at the rates obtainable at the mines or in the towns. Moreover, at those seasons of the year when he needs most labour, and needs it most urgently, he invariably finds it most difficult to secure. When he wants to plough his land or reap his crops, the natives are engaged in similar work at their kraals, and are naturally unwilling to go out to labour. At these seasons, too, the competition of other farmers for native labourers is most active, and they are least willing to allow labour to be recruited from their tenants. In the east of Cape Colony this difficulty is

sometimes met by gangs of native sheep-shearers and harvesters, who go from farm to farm as their services are required, and many farmers in that colony still prefer to rely entirely on volunteer labour.

But the increasing demand for natives at the mines, on the railways, and in the towns has made this system of working the farms more and more precarious, and most farmers now obtain much of their labour from natives living on their farms. Owing to the enormous size of most of the farms, the farmer is often unable to work the whole of his land, and therefore finds it convenient to allow parties of natives to settle on it on condition that they work for him when he requires their services. Natives whose tribes have been broken up in war, or who have desired to escape from the capricious authority of their chiefs, have often been glad to find a home with the farmer on these terms. The arrangements between the farmers and these labour-tenants vary considerably on different farms. The farmer allows them land to cultivate and grazing for their cattle, for which he sometimes charges a small rent, and in some cases he lends them cattle for ploughing, or ploughs their land for them, if they desire it. The labour-tenants, on their side, undertake that they or their sons will work for the farmer at a low wage when required during part of the year; and they are sometimes employed by the farmer during other parts of the year as voluntary labourers. They are not, however, as a rule, at liberty to seek work elsewhere without the farmer's consent. On many farms the labour-tenants occupy their land on a sort of metayer tenancy known as "ploughing on halves" or "thirds," the tenant handing over to the farmer a half or a third of the produce of the land which he cultivates. This system is only practicable on farms with a considerable acreage of cultivatable land, but it appears to be popular with the natives and remunerative to the farmers. The system of labour-tenancy has undoubtedly done much to meet the requirements both of the farmer and the natives, and, when the arrangements between them are clearly defined and the contracts are made with the tenants themselves, it often works satisfactorily enough. But it frequently happens that farmers are content to rely on vague verbal arrangements of doubtful validity, often made with the heads of kraals, and in these cases disputes constantly arise as to the terms of the tenancies. In Natal the magistrate's court is sometimes "inundated" with cases of this kind, and the friction between landlords and tenants in that.colony is said to be "daily becoming more acute." Moreover, in many districts labour-tenancy has developed into almost unlimited "squatting," and the supply of available labour is seriously restricted by farmers keeping an excessive number of natives practically tied to their land even when their services are not required. The squatters are an unprogressive class, and many farmers, from fear of stock-thieving, strongly object to them as neighbours. The practice of squatting retards the advance of the natives and leads to many difficulties, and it undoubtedly encourages absentee landlordism and incompetent farming. So serious are these drawbacks to the system that the Natal Native Affairs Commission recommended that the law should recognise only two classes of farm occupants, the servant and the tenant, the servant paying no rent, and the tenant being free to dispose of his labour.

The census returns show that in 1904 there were about 135,000 Bantu natives, and about 58,000 coloured persons of "mixed and other" races employed on farms in Cape Colony, the Transvaal, the Orange River Colony and Southern Rhodesia ; and to these figures must be added a large proportion of the 40,000 labourers similarly employed in Natal. These numbers would no doubt be

considerably increased if squatting were judiciously restricted and farm labourers could depend on receiving a
fair wage and considerate treatment.   On the other hand,
most farm labourers are extremely inefficient.   They are
accustomed to primitive methods of cultivation, and little
trouble is generally taken to train them for their work.
The Director of the Natal census pointed out that there
were 13.4 hands employed on the farms in that colony to
every hundred acres in crops, as against 5.38 hands generally
required for the effective ordinary cultivation of that area in
England ; and the majority of the Transvaal Labour Commission of 1903, in estimating the labour requirements of
the Transvaal farms, adopted a basis of one native to every
three acres.   These figures indicate a lack of labour-saving
machinery and the inefficiency of farm labour.   More progressive methods of farming are greatly needed, both to
economise the labour supply and to increase the agricultural
output of the country, but they are impracticable so long
as farmers are content to rely on untrained and indifferent
labourers.   For their own benefit they would do well to
take a more active interest in the instruction and welfare
of their employees, for with proper training many natives
make excellent labourers.   In a communication addressed
to this Committee, Mr. Livingstone Moffat, a farmer of
long standing in the Eastern Province, writes :

> There is a most striking contrast between the
> average location Kafir and the average native who
> has lived for some years on a farm : the former is as
> impudent as the latter is civil ; the one is a loafer and
> skulker at work besides being, as a rule, inefficient ;
> the other one cannot but respect when one sees how
> he can handle his spade or team. . . .
> The thoroughly well-bred Matabeles (said Mr.
> E. A. Hull, a farmer in Rhodesia, when giving
> evidence before the Native Affairs Commission) can
> really be taught anything.   In my experience with
> natives I have found that every farmer who deals with

them has to pay as much attention to them as to his team of bullocks, that is, he has to select the wheelers and the leaders. You find some boys, especially the "Amazansi" (that is the pure-bred), who will learn anything, from driving teams to working machinery, and the more responsibility you put on them the better they are. Others you find exactly the reverse, and as soon as you put them in a responsible position they abuse it immediately. I may say that personally I have been very successful. Although people will tell you that the Matabele will not stay with you, I have boys who have remained with me for seven years, all the time I have been in the country, and who are absolutely capable men to-day, though they were perfectly raw when I started with them.

But too often the necessary instruction is neglected, and the farmer seeks to increase the number of his employees rather than to improve the quality of their work.

Progressive, up-to-date farming (writes Mr. Livingstone Moffat) is the exception, and primitive methods requiring large numbers of hands, instead of labour-saving machinery, the rule. . . . Native labour has been used because it was the only kind available, and till of late in any quantity. The mistake has been not to improve the quality. The crying need is Education and the discouraging of the squatting system outside native reserves. There is a grand future (he adds) in the agricultural and pastoral development of South Africa, but it is not going to be accomplished by uncivilised natives, working in their crude and primitive fashion. So long as there is the present tendency to leave agriculture in the hands of natives, who are uneducated, shiftless, and ignorant of the first principles of agriculture, and have never learned habits of industry, so long will that development be postponed, and capital will seek other spheres which promise to employ greater intelligence and more scientific methods in the direction and employment of labour as a means of production.

During recent years there has been a striking increase in Cape Colony in the number of natives and coloured persons

who have become farmers on their own account. In 1904
out of the 40,942 farmers in that Colony 3,544 were Bantu
natives and 3,008 were coloured people of " mixed or other "
races. In Natal there were 166 coloured farmers (including
assistants), and a number of natives in that Colony have
been purchasing land ; but the exact number of native
farmers has not been ascertained. In the Orange River
Colony there were 416 native and 37 coloured farmers ; but
in the Transvaal there were no native farmers and only 43
coloured.

Native farmers are not unfrequently joint-owners of land
which they have subscribed to purchase, but considerable
prices are sometimes paid for farms by individual natives.
A witness before the Native Affairs Commission stated :
" I sold a farm to a native for £2,000 in the Komgha district not very long ago, and I had £1,600 offered to me for
a farm in the Peddie district by a native less than a fortnight ago, who was prepared to put down the money.
A year ago I sold a quit-rent farm in the Stutterheim district to a native for £750. I could give further instances."
A good many colonists regard the advent of the native
farmer with considerable apprehension, and the majority
of the Native Affairs Commission were of opinion that the
natives' right to purchase land ought to be restricted to
certain prescribed areas and that land so purchased should
not be communally occupied. Some of the farms owned by
natives are little better than locations of squatters, and
farms of this kind ought no doubt to be confined to suitable districts. But other native farms are of a different
character, and no sufficient reason seems to have been given
for placing difficulties in the way of those natives who
by their industry and thrift are able to purchase land and
are prepared to occupy it in an unobjectionable manner.

A striking instance of the interest which some of the

[1] Native Affairs Commission, 1903-5, Q. 8619.

natives are beginning to take in the improvement of their agriculture occurs in the report of Mr. W. T. Brownlee, the Resident Magistrate for the District of Butterworth, for 1906. " A few of the more progressive natives of this district," he writes, " have, during the year, started an Agricultural Society, which has for its main object the improvement of methods of agriculture and farming generally. I hope to see this Society grow, and, because its inception and birth are entirely spontaneous, I believe it will be of great benefit to the people of this district."

(c) Mining

Unlike the agriculture of South Africa, the great gold mining industries of the country have been developed with extraordinary rapidity, and they now provide by far the most important of the industrial occupations of the natives. But in a land of conservative habits the enterprising methods of the mine-owners have been somewhat disturbing anomalies. It has in consequence been extremely difficult to readjust the economic conditions fast enough to meet their requirements ; and in their relations with the natives this difficulty has unfortunately become exceptionally acute. Although the natives are steadily becoming more industrious and great numbers of them seek employment at the mines, the rapid expansion of these industries has inevitably put an excessive strain on the available supply of labourers, and has made the labour question one of the most insistent and perplexing of South African problems. In their anxiety to force the pace the mine-owners have not always been patient or reasonable in their demands, and they have sometimes advocated measures, such as the imposition of labour taxes, which it is impossible to justify. Undoubtedly, however, in obtaining labour for their vast and progressive undertakings they have a task of unusual difficulty. Many natives have a strong dislike to underground work ; those who come to the mines from British South Africa generally stay only for a few months and have continually to be replaced ; and in many cases the labourers have to be recruited from great distances without adequate means of transport.   To overcome these difficulties it has been necessary to organise an elaborate system of recruiting, to provide facilities for travelling to and from the mines, and to offer exceptionally attractive terms of employment.   It has also been necessary to guard the natives from fraud and ill-treatment and to devise and enforce hygienic precautions to protect them from the diseases to which when employed underground they are peculiarly liable.   In all these directions important progress has been made during the last few years, and some of the improvements which have been effected are sufficiently noteworthy to claim at least a brief examination.

At the close of the year 1901 important measures were taken by the Transvaal Government to place the recruiting and employment of natives for the Rand mines on a more satisfactory basis.   Recruiting was restricted, as in the other colonies, to properly licensed labour agents, who were made liable to heavy penalties for misconduct.   Licences were required for all compound overseers in the labour districts who had charge of fifty or more natives.   The pass system was made less onerous, and pass officers were required to ascertain that natives in charge of labour agents understood the terms of their contracts and had entered into them voluntarily.   Contracts of employment for more than a year were made illegal, unless sanctioned by the Native Com-missioner.   The punishment of flogging for desertion and offences against the pass laws was abolished.   And, to en-sure the proper treatment of the natives while in employ-ment, a number of Inspectors of Natives in the labour districts were appointed in the following year to inquire into and redress or report grievances, to deal with breaches of discipline and minor contraventions of official regulations, and to settle disputes between natives of a civil nature. By these measures a fairly adequate system of official supervision seems to have been established for the protection of natives both in making and carrying out their contracts, and the Native Department has been thereby enabled to keep in touch with the natives in their employments and to deal with any legitimate grievances. A further reform of the utmost importance was effected by the prohibition, under severe penalties, of the supply of intoxicants to any coloured person. The supply of Kafir beer by employers was subsequently legalised, but the excessive drinking which used to prevail on the Rand seems to have been effectually checked. A grave danger to the natives has thus been removed, and the efficiency of their labour greatly increased.

Facilities of a very useful kind have been provided for the safe custody and transmission of the natives' earnings. Before the late war the Governments of Cape Colony, Natal, and Basutoland had established separate agencies at Johannesburg to enable natives on the Rand to remit money to their homes. As these offices had been much appreciated by the natives, the Transvaal Government in 1902 opened a general Deposit and Remittance Agency, under the Native Affairs Department, at Johannesburg, and subsequently established branch offices at Pretoria and Germiston. Until 1906 the other Governments contributed to its support, but in that year the Natal Government withdrew from the arrangement,[1] and the agency was transferred to the Postal Department. Considerable sums are received and transmitted by the agency, the remittances during the year ending June 30, 1906, amounting to £29,194, the deposits to £10,855, the withdrawals to £10,426, and £6,500 being held at the end

[1] In 1907 the Natal Government established a separate agency.

of the year on fixed deposit bearing interest. The agency
has been of great assistance to the natives as a means of
communicating with their families and friends, as their
kraals are often out of reach of the ordinary post. It is
thus in various ways an extremely useful institution, and
it is to be hoped that magistrates and district officials will
encourage natives to take advantage of it. In addition
to this agency, the Transvaal Government in 1906 established a Native Labour Bureau for the reception, medical
examination, and registration of natives recruited for the
Rand from British South Africa. It is understood that
this bureau is not a recruiting agency, but it should prove
a valuable institution both to the natives and their employers.
A fee of 2s. 6d. is charged for each native who passes through
the bureau.

The mine-owners have done much during recent years
to make the position of their employees more satisfactory.
But for some time after the war they had great difficulty
in obtaining an adequate supply of natives. This was
partly due to the increasing demand for labour at high
wages in other industries, and to the fact that many
natives, owing to their large earnings during the war, were
for a time indisposed to leave their homes. But the difficulty
was certainly aggravated by the injudicious action of the
mine-owners in reducing the rate of wages. On the ground
that the wages paid on the Rand before the war were
excessive, the rates were in 1900 reduced by about a third.
The dissatisfaction of the natives at this step undoubtedly
tended to discourage them from seeking employment at
this centre. The old rates were restored in 1903. But
for some time afterwards a feeling of uncertainty as to
wages continued among the natives, and the return to the
higher rates did not at once lead to any great increase in
the supply of labour. During these years the position on
the Rand became extremely critical. The mine-owners

represented that the available native labour in South Africa was insufficient for their needs, and claimed that it should be supplemented by the introduction of Chinese coolies. This proposal evoked a vigorous opposition. It was urged that the labour resources of the country had not been exhausted ; that whites, as well as natives, could with advantage be employed even for unskilled work, and that the requirements of the mines had been exaggerated. The complicated character of these questions called for careful investigation, and in 1903 the Transvaal Labour Commission was appointed to inquire into the possibility of meeting the labour requirements of the Colony from Central and Southern Africa. This Commission reported " that the demand for native labour for the Transvaal mining industry is in excess of the present supply by about 129,000 labourers ; and, whilst no complete data of the future requirements of the whole industry are obtainable, it is estimated that the mines of the Witwatersrand alone will require, within the next five years, an additional supply of 196,000 labourers." It also found that there was a large deficiency of labour for the agriculture, railways and other industries of the Colony ; that there was no adequate supply of labour in Central and Southern Africa to meet these requirements, and that the use of white unskilled labour had not been shown to be practicable. Two of the Commissioners, however, presented a minority report, in which they strongly protested against these conclusions, and maintained that 115,250 labourers should be sufficient for the gold and coal mines. The report of the Commission was followed in 1904 by an ordinance legalising the importation of Chinese coolies for employment at the mines under stringent conditions, precluding them from engaging in other occupations and ensuring their repatriation on the termination of their contracts. By the end of that year about 20,000 coolies were at work on the Rand, and in December 1906 the number had risen to 52,917. But at the end of 1905 the Imperial Government had prohibited any further importations, unless already contracted for, and after the grant of self-government to the Colony the Transvaal Government decided that the employment of Chinese labourers in the mines should cease "at the earliest possible moment." The coolies are therefore being steadily repatriated as their contracts expire. At the end of 1907 there were still 35,676 coolies in the employment of the mining companies, but 24,016 of these were to return to China during the present year.

The introduction of the Chinese has been an important factor in the labour question on the Rand ; but the consideration of this much-debated subject lies outside the scope of the present volume. The experiment may have served a temporary purpose. It was, however, open to grave objections. It provoked bitter and wide-spread controversies. It brought into South Africa a new and unwelcome racial difficulty, and from many points of view it is well that it is not to be continued.

The mine-owners have now to rely on measures for increasing the supply and efficiency of native labour, and they have already done much to make the conditions of employment on the mines more attractive to the natives. The rates of wages have been raised. The compounds in which the natives are accommodated, and to which they are confined at night after 9 p.m., have been made more commodious and sanitary. Special care is taken to provide good and sufficient food, the rations generally including meat, vegetables and Kafir beer twice a week, besides the daily allowance of mealies, biscuits, coffee and lime-juice. The mealie food to which the natives are accustomed is, however, extremely cheap, and even with these improvements the average monthly cost of the raw material for food and medical attendance for coloured employees on the

Transvaal gold mines during 1905–6 was only 7s. per head. In consequence of complaints of ill-treatment from some of the Cape Colony natives, the Cape Government in 1903 sent Mr. W. T. Brownlee, with a number of headmen from native districts, to inquire into the condition and treatment of natives working at and near Johannesburg. This deputation made a careful investigation with, on the whole, satisfactory results. The food was found to be " sufficient and wholesome," and the compounds fairly comfortable ; and there were few complaints of serious ill-treatment. But it was noticed that almost all the native overseers carried sjamboks, which in some cases appeared to be used freely, and complaints were made of misunderstandings as to the rates of wages and of the misrepresentations of labour agents. Steps have, however, been taken by the Native Affairs Department and the mine-owners to remedy these grievances. Overseers found guilty of assaults on natives have been punished ; ,the licences of labour agents convicted of misrepresentations have been cancelled : and, to avoid misunderstandings as to wages, natives have been registered at a daily rate of pay. Better arrangements have also been made for their transport by rail, and rest-houses have been provided on various routes for their accommodation. In 1906 Mr. Brownlee, accompanied by Mr. A. H. Stanford, again visited Johannesburg on behalf of the Cape Government, and reported that at the compounds which they inspected, with one exception, the labourers were " well treated and well fed," and spoke in high terms of their managers. There were, however, complaints of the conduct of the native overseers, and, at one mine, of ill-treatment by white miners underground.

It is satisfactory to note that during the last few years there has been a marked improvement in the health of the natives working on the Rand. In a memorandum of

the Native Affairs Department in March 1904[1] it was
stated that " a striking testimony to the favourable terms
and general hygienic conditions under which natives are
at present employed on the mines is to be found in the
contrast in health, physical fitness, and general appearance
between natives arriving and those returning to their
homes. Many come to work in a more or less emaciated
condition, but few leave who are not in robust health and
have not reaped the benefits of regular work, better food
and better living conditions than they are accustomed
to in their own homes." That the hygiene on these
mines requires most careful attention has long been evident
from the high mortality among the natives who work on
them. In February 1904 Lord Milner informed the
Colonial Secretary that " the high rate of mortality in
mines is the weakest point in our armour, and though
mining can never be a healthy employment, the death-rate
ought to be enormously reduced." During the preceding
year (1903) the average death-rate had been no less than
71·25 per thousand ; and, although this appalling figure
may have been partly due to the incautious employment of
natives of poor physique, there is little doubt that it was
largely to be attributed to defective accommodation and the
neglect of necessary precautions. Since that date great
efforts have been made by the Native Affairs Department
and the mine-owners to reduce the mortality to a more
normal rate. Outbreaks of scurvy have been checked by
providing lime-juice and vegetables as regular articles of
diet, and the still greater danger from pneumonia and other
pulmonary diseases has been guarded against by erecting
change houses at shaft heads, by supplying the natives
with coats or blankets when leaving work, and by other

[1] See Transvaal Blue Book containing *Correspondence relating to
Conditions of Native Labour employed in the Transvaal Mines* (Col.
2025), p. 66.

necessary precautions. Improvements have been made in
the lighting, ventilation, and sanitary arrangements of
the compounds, and a number of hospitals have been
provided, some of which are said to be excellent. Recruits
are subjected to medical examination before they are
engaged. The introduction of natives from north of
latitude 22° during the winter months has been prohibited.
Carefully considered regulations as to diet, accommodation
and other matters have been promulgated under the
Coloured Labourers' Health Regulations Ordinance of 1905.
These measures have had a most salutary effect. In the
year 1905–6 the death-rate among the natives in the mines
had fallen to 45·541 per thousand ; in the following year it
showed a further decline to 34·020 ; and in 1907 it was
31·724. This remarkable improvement may well encourage the mine-owners and the officials of the Native Affairs
Department to continue to give this important matter their
vigilant attention. A majority of the mining companies
have now voluntarily adopted a scheme for providing
compensation for accidents to natives, and in 1905–6 a total
amount of £4,942 17s. 9d. was distributed to the bene-
ficiaries. The Native Affairs Department has drawn the
attention of other large employers to the advantages of an
arrangement of this kind, and its representations are
stated to have been received sympathetically.

Before the year 1900 no adequate organisation existed
for collecting the immense force of native labourers
required on the Rand. But in that year, in order to avoid
competition for labour between the numerous companies
and to prevent the employment of incompetent or un-
scrupulous labour agents, the Rand Native Labour
Association was reconstructed under the name of the
Witwatersrand Native Labour Association, with wide
powers to recruit and distribute natives for the mines.
Each company that joined the Association received the

quota of natives to which it was entitled under the
articles of association, but it was prohibited from employing
natives independently. Nearly all the mining companies
became members, and a great recruiting monopoly was
thus established. This powerful body, with its great
influence and ample funds, has now established a wide-
spread and carefully devised system of collecting labour.
Its returns for 1907 show that in that year it succeeded in
obtaining no fewer than 100,082 natives from the following
sources :

Transvaal	6,233
Swaziland	80
Bechuanaland	1
Cape Colony	5,201
Basutoland and Orange River Colony . .	1,858
British Central Africa Protectorate . . .	488
Province of Mozambique	47,656
Local	38,565
Total	100,082

For every native imported from the Portuguese territories
of Mozambique a sum of 13s. is payable to the Portuguese
Government, and a further sum of 10s. has to be paid to
the Government by the native on his return for each year
of his service. A charge of 6d. per month has also to be paid
by the employer of any Mozambique native who has changed
his employment or re-engaged. Notwithstanding these im-
posts, the Association has found the province of Mozambique
by far the most productive and satisfactory of its recruiting
grounds. The natives from these territories are engaged
on twelve months' contracts, at a wage of 1s. 6d. per day,
and they seem to have no strong dislike to underground
work, as they frequently renew their contracts for a further
six months.[1] These Portuguese natives must, therefore,

[1] See the speech of the Chairman of the Witwatersrand Native
Labour Supply Association at the annual meeting on March 29, 1906.

year by year, be taking home considerable earnings, and
it would be particularly interesting to know what effects
are being produced in the kraals of Mozambique by this
influx of wealth. In British Central Africa and Rhodesia
natives are engaged on the same or similar terms. For
natives from the Transvaal, Swaziland, Bechuanaland,
Cape Colony, Basutoland and the Orange River Colony
the rate of pay is 2s. per day for underground work, and
1s. 8d. per day for surface work, subject to the recognised
task of the mine being performed. In the case of these
natives a six months' contract has been adopted, but Cape
Colony natives may engage for four months on agreeing to
refund 25s. for their railway fare, Bechuanaland and West
Transvaal natives for three months, and East Transvaal
natives for four months, on agreeing to repay 10s. towards
their fare. The rates of pay mentioned above represent
the maximum paid for unskilled work, but much higher
rates are paid for work involving skill or responsibility.
Some of the native employees on the Rand earn as much
as £4 or £5 a month, and a native compound manager
informed the Native Affairs Commission that he was
receiving £26 10s. per month.[1] With the exceptions
mentioned above, the Association pays all railway fares,
Government dues and other expenses incurred in bringing
the natives to the mines, and it has expended considerable
sums in providing depôts and rest-houses. It employs a
large number of licensed labour agents and a host of
native runners, who go from kraal to kraal inviting the
natives to come out to work, and guide those who wish
to do so to the rest-houses and camps of the Association.
Before proceeding to the Rand, natives engaged by an
agent enter into contracts before a Government official,
and, if a doctor is available, they are medically examined,
and those who are physically unfit are sent home. As

[1] The Native Affairs Commission 1903-5.—Qs. 44, 431-2.

soon as an agent has collected a gang of labourers he sends them to the Association's depôt at Johannesburg. From some districts, owing to the absence of railways, the whole or part of the journey has to be accomplished on foot, and along such routes the Association has provided rest-houses, where the natives can obtain shelter and food at the end of each day's march. Natives who come from the warmer districts, and consequently wear little clothing, are supplied with clothes, the cost of which is recovered from their wages; and small advances are sometimes made to enable natives to pay their taxes before leaving home. On arriving at the depôt at Johannesburg they are supplied with food, and, when necessary, with extra blankets. In wet or cold weather fires are provided. After twenty-four hours' detention in the depôt they are medically examined, and those who are found to be fit for work are sent on to their employers. Some of those who arrive in a weak condition are detained in the compound until they are passed by the doctor. The others are returned to their homes, unless they are seriously ill and desire to remain in the Association's hospital. Sick natives often wish to return home at once, and care seems to be taken in these cases to provide escorts and medical attendance when necessary.

In consequence of the high mortality among the natives obtained from the British Central Africa Protectorate, the Imperial Government has prohibited the employment of these natives on the Rand. The Association is no longer able to obtain natives from Rhodesia, as the Rhodesian Government, in view of the increasing local demand for labour, has prohibited recruiting in that country for the Transvaal mines. On the other hand, recruiting in Natal, which had been prohibited, was legalised in January 1908.

The monopoly of recruiting vested in the Association

has been severely criticised, and it has been represented that the supply of natives for the mines could be greatly increased if the companies were at liberty to recruit independently. In deference to these views, or to test their accuracy, the Association decided in 1906 to relax the prohibition against separate recruiting by its members ; and the various companies are now at liberty to collect natives on their own account. No company, however, may offer a higher wage than 2s. per day for underground and 1s. 8d. per day for surface work ; and all natives engaged in this way have to be registered with the Association. During 1907 the independent recruiters succeeded in collecting 17,909 natives, of whom 11,799 were obtained in Cape Colony. The Association withdrew some of its agents to avoid competing with its own members ; but, as it recruited only 4,055 natives from Cape Colony during 1906, and 5,201 during 1907, it would seem that for the natives of that colony the independent system of recruiting was the more successful.

In addition to the natives recruited by the Association and the companies, many natives come direct to the Rand. In 1907 no fewer than 19,237 of the natives described as "local" in the returns of the Association were really labourers who had thus found their own way to the mines. Natives from the more progressive districts who can afford to pay their fares often prefer to come to industrial centres in this manner, as by so doing they avoid entering into contracts beforehand and are free to arrange terms with their employers on the spot. This practice, which is particularly popular with some of the Cape Colony natives, saves the employer the expense of recruiting ; and in the interests of both parties every facility should be given to natives to seek employment in this way.

The total number of natives in the employment of members of the Association (exclusive of the Barberton district, but including 9,009 natives employed in collieries) on December 31, 1907, was 106,290, showing an increase of 25,059 during the year.   By the end of September 1908 the number had risen to no fewer than 136,180, but the latter figure includes the natives employed by the J. B. Robinson group of companies, who left the Association in 1906, but rejoined it in January 1908.   This group at the date of rejoining had 9,580 natives in its employ, exclusive of natives engaged by contractors.   The Barberton members of the Association were employing 2,294 natives at the end of 1907, and a considerable number of natives are working for gold-mining companies which have not joined the Association.

Although the gold-mining companies of the Transvaal have failed until recently to recruit natives as rapidly as had been hoped, the increase in their output has been enormous.   In eleven years the value of the gold which they produce annually has risen from £8,603,831 in 1896 to the astonishing figure of £27,403,738 (representing 6,451,384 ounces) in 1907.   The labour troubles which have arisen have been the natural consequence of this rapid expansion, and difficulties of this kind will no doubt have to be faced in the future.   But the energy and knowledge which are now being brought to bear on the solution of this question, and the attention which is being given to the use of labour-saving appliances augur well for the success of the mine-owners in obtaining sufficient labour for their purposes, notwithstanding the repatriation of the Chinese coolies.

The demand for labour on the Rand has caused some anxiety on the gold mines of Southern Rhodesia.   For these mines, though on a small scale as compared with the gigantic industry on the Rand, have of late been making rapid progress.   In 1899 their output of gold was only 56,742 ounces, but in 1907 it had risen to 612,053 ounces ;

and this development has greatly increased the need of labour. In winter the supply seems to be fairly satisfactory; but during the months when the natives are cultivating their fields and reaping their crops, even the offer of higher wages often fails to induce them to leave their kraals. The Chief Native Commissioner of Matabeleland reported that at the beginning of the year 1905–6 8,955 natives were employed in mining, and that the number rose during the year to 10,763, the supply of labour being in excess of the demand during the months of April, May, and June, but falling short subsequently. In his opinion, " much can be done to increase the supply," and he draws attention to the fact that " in those mines where operations have been continuous, and qualified compound managers are employed, no difficulty is experienced in maintaining their full complement of boys." In consequence of the complaints of scarcity of labour, the Administrator appointed a committee during that year to investigate the subject, and in accordance with the recommendations of this committee, the Rhodesian Native Labour Bureau was reconstituted, and, to provide it with funds, employers were required to pay a monthly registration fee of 2s. for every native labourer over the age of fourteen engaged in any form of mining work. The natives seem to have been usually engaged by monthly contracts, and the committee recommended lengthening the term of employment in order to distribute labour more equally throughout the year. They also advised the adoption of a standard scale of rations and a minimum wage, the exemption from taxation of natives who had been in *bonâ fide* and continuous employment for twelve months, and the imposition of rent on natives living outside the reserves on unalienated lands of the British South Africa Company.

The wages paid on the Rhodesian mines appear to be considerably lower than those on the Rand. The Native

Affairs Commission were informed by Colonel Grey, the
representative of the Salisbury Chamber of Mines, that the
average wage might be taken roughly at from 36s. to 38s.
a month, and the maximum at about £3 10s. with food.
The accommodation for natives on the Rhodesian mines,
although not perfect, has been improved, and attention has
been given to sanitation, diet, and medical attendance.   By
effecting further improvements in these directions, the mine-
owners could probably do much to increase the number
and efficiency of their employees.   Recruiting for these
mines is carried on by private agents and by the Rhodesian
Native Labour Bureau.   The Bureau, as a responsible
organisation able to ensure proper treatment of its recruits,
is well supported by the Government.   It has been largely
engaged in collecting labour in North-Eastern and North-
Western Rhodesia, and apparently with considerable success.   Natives from the former district usually contract
for terms of twelve months; those from the latter for six
months, with the option to renew their contracts for three
months longer.

Next in importance among the industrial employers of
natives are the diamond and coal-mining companies.   During the year 1906–7 the average number of coloured
employees on the diamond mines of the Transvaal was
7,697 ; about 4,000 appear to be engaged in diamond-mining
in the Orange River Colony ; 23,769 were employed on an
average in 1906–7 by the De Beers Company at Kimberley ; and a comparatively small but probably increasing
number are now apparently engaged in the production
of diamonds in Rhodesia.   The wages paid by the
diamond mines are exceptionally high.   At Kimberley the
ordinary rate has been 15s. a week, but the natives have often
been able to earn from 20s. to 25s.   Owing to the necessity
for guarding against theft, and in order to prevent the
natives from obtaining intoxicants, the De Beers' compound

system is of an extremely stringent kind. The natives are confined strictly to the compound enclosure, and are subjected to a somewhat rigorous discipline. But Mr. G. W. Barnes, the Protector of Natives, reports that " they are comfortably housed, and everything done to make their lives as pleasant as possible." Large sums have been expended in improving the compounds, and the fact that these mines have little difficulty in obtaining labour is good evidence of the satisfactory treatment of their employees.[1] The diamond-mining companies have of late greatly reduced the number of their hands; and this to some extent accounts for the large increase in the number of natives recruited for the Rand.

The number of natives employed in the coal mines is also very considerable. According to the census returns, 2,173 natives were so employed in Cape Colony, and over 900 in the Orange River Colony. The report of the Transvaal Government Mining Engineer for 1906–7 shows that 10,387 coloured persons were employed in the collieries of that colony at the end of June 1907 ; and the representative of the Natal Mine Managers' Association informed the Native Affairs Commission that the mines included in that Association were employing over 3,000 natives. The number employed in the Rhodesian coal mines would no doubt be comparatively small. The average monthly wage on the Transvaal coal mines in 1906–7 was 43s. 2d. In Natal experienced men working underground earn from £2 to £4 a month, and others from 30s. to 50s. per month, with food and lodging. Considerable improvements are stated to have been made both in the diet and the accommodation provided on the Natal mines ; and the Natal Native Affairs Commission specially refers to " the splen-

---

[1] The Kimberley Compound System is fully described in the volume edited by this Committee, entitled " The Natives of South Africa " (John Murray), p. 139 et seq.

did example set by the Newcastle Colliery in providing
decent cottages for married natives, and paying them
good wages" as an instance of "what can be done by
studying mutuality of interest." On the Indwe mines in
Cape Colony the wage has been about 2s. a day, in
addition to food and accommodation ; and these mines
seem to have been well supplied with labour. By providing
land for occupation by their employees the Indwe Company have been able to induce many of its more efficient
natives to settle with their families near the mines and
to give their services for about fifteen days in each month.
With proper supervision this plan has great advantages,
and it is worthy of consideration whether it should not be
adopted more widely. This company has also made the
experiment of employing female labour, apparently with
success.

(d) Other Industrial and Commercial and Domestic Employments

Many natives are engaged in unskilled work on the
railways, roads, docks and other public works, as assistants
in stores, and in many other occupations under private
employers. During recent years, owing to the great
demand for labour, they have often been earning high
wages. A few illustrations will show approximately the
usual rates. In Cape Town the dock labourers receive
4s. a day with 9d. an hour extra for overtime ; and from
4s. to 5s. seems to be the usual pay for an ordinary unskilled labourer. In other towns from 2s. to 3s. a day
seems to be about the usual wage, but higher rates are
frequently paid, and some of the experienced dock hands
at the seaports are said to get as much as 7s. or 8s. a day.
Labourers on the Cape Railway, who sometimes remain
for years, receive from 3s. to 4s. 6d. a day and are provided

with rough accommodation; those on the Central South African Railways, who are engaged on six months' contracts, receive 1s. 8d. a day and food, and "boss-boys" or indunas 2s. 6d. to 3s. a day with food. Store boys in towns can earn from 30s. to £3 a month, with food, but in country districts they are sometimes paid not more than 1s. a day. In employments which involve skilled work or the discharge of responsible duties much higher remuneration is given. In the Cape postal service, for instance, linesmen receive about £80 a year, letter-carriers from £70 to £100, with £5 a year for overtime, and telegraph messengers from £60 to £100.

The practice of employing natives and coloured people as domestic servants is a fact of special importance in the social economy of South Africa, both on account of the close relations which it involves between the two races and because the number of servants is exceedingly large. The census returns of 1904 showed that in Cape Colony, the Transvaal, and the Orange River Colony, over 117,000 natives and coloured persons were employed in this capacity, of whom about 40,000 were males and 77,000 females. Were these servants carefully trained by their employers and prepared for such training by a judicious education, this system of domestic service might work well enough. In that case its effects on the natives might be as beneficial as they are undoubtedly far-reaching. But many domestic servants have had no such training or education, and their employment is not seldom a source of mischief both to themselves and to the families for whom they work. The wages paid to domestic servants vary greatly in different parts of the country. Cooks sometimes earn as much as 8s. a day, but in Cape Town, Pretoria, and Johannesburg from £2 10s. to £4 a month, with food and lodging, seems to be the usual wage, and in some districts the house-boys only receive about

15*s.* to £1 and the girls from 10*s.* to 15*s.* a month, in addition to their food and lodging.

A number of natives are now learning trades at various institutions, and many who have been thus trained are capable, under the supervision of Europeans, of doing good work. A case was mentioned before the Native Affairs Commission of a native saddler who was making £250 a year,[1] but as a rule the earnings of native artisans seem to range from about £5 to £8 a month, and most of them do not possess sufficient capital or skill to work successfully on their own account. Native workmen with some technical skill are much needed in South Africa, but unfortunately they are often regarded with jealousy by the white artisans, who have an excessive dread of their competition. In consequence of this feeling native artisans have sometimes had difficulty in obtaining employment. Building contractors, it is stated, have refused to engage them for skilled work, and at Bloemfontein their employment in carpentry or building in connection with town work is forbidden by a municipal by-law. At present the demand for the services of the native artisan among his own people is very limited, and in native districts like Basutoland natives who have received an industrial training sometimes carry on their trades merely as useful adjuncts to their ordinary agricultural occupations. But the need for their work among the natives is steadily increasing, and in time it should provide them with ample employment.

It is greatly to be regretted that municipal authorities have often omitted to make any adequate provision for the accommodation and supervision of the natives who now flock to the towns in search of work. The consequences of this neglect have been deplorable in the extreme. It has exposed the natives to temptations which they are wholly

[1] The Native Affairs Commission, 1903-5.—Q. 39, 550.

unfitted to resist, and too many of them have been utterly demoralised by the vices and licence of town life. How serious these evils have become may be gathered from the reports of magistrates and other officials, who have watched with growing anxiety the far-reaching effects of this fatal contamination. To take a single instance—Mr. Stuart, the First Assistant-Magistrate of Durban, draws attention, in his report for 1904, to the growth among the younger natives of a new spirit of lawlessness. He describes them as losing their good manners, showing less respect to elders, and becoming quarrelsome and churlish. Immorality, he states, is increasing, and the practice of divorce, formerly unknown, is now common. This demoralisation he traces directly to the lack of necessary safeguards and restrictions in the relations between the two races.

The need for proper supervision of the natives in the towns is the greater on account of the growing number of day labourers or "togt"[1] men, who by their large earnings are independent of settled occupations. At some of the chief towns large locations for natives have now been provided. Thus the labourer who comes to Cape Town for employment is lodged at the Harbour Board location for 8s. a month, if he works at the dock ; or, if he wishes to work in the town, he can sleep at the Maitland location, where cottages can be obtained for £2 and lean-to huts for 10s. a month. In the East London and Kimberley locations small pieces of land are let to the natives at 2s. a month and 10s. a quarter respectively, on which they erect their huts. In the new Johannesburg location buildings are let to natives at a reasonable monthly rent, and a cheap train service has been established. Considerable care seems to have been taken to ensure the efficient

[1] The "togt" labourer in Durban has to take out a monthly licence, for which the fee is 5s.

management of some of these town locations, but too
many of the locations provided by municipalities for native
labourers appear to be extremely defective both as regards
management and accommodation, and even in so important
a centre as Durban, notwithstanding the erection some
years ago of a barracks for " togt " men, the housing arrangements for natives seem still to be very inadequate. The
Superintendent of Police informed the Native Affairs
Commission that the barracks provided accommodation
only for about 2,500 out of the 7,500 " togt " men in the
town, and he pointed out the urgent need for a proper
location. The merchants, he said, did " not require any
natives in the town proper after 5 p.m., except waiters.
Stores are closed at five. Natives are left in the yard till
six the next morning. Between nine p.m. and six a.m.
they are shut up like rats in a hole, and cannot get out.
That is what I complain of. Some of these backyards
are not fit for dogs, let alone human beings."

(e) Professional Occupations

A number of natives are employed as policemen and
interpreters, and as intermediate and subordinate officials
in various Government departments ; many have become
ministers or teachers, and there are a few native editors
of newspapers ; but there is little opening for the native
in other professional occupations, and at present only
exceptional natives are qualified for such positions. There
will, no doubt, in time be an increasing demand among the
natives themselves for native lawyers, doctors, and nurses ;
but hitherto the native who has received an education
much above the average is too apt to find himself unable
to turn it to account, and is naturally disposed to resent
the false position in which he is thus placed. Hitherto a
large proportion of the better educated natives have been

trained by the various missionary societies as teachers, evangelists, and ministers, and many of them are doing good and responsible work in these capacities.

The status of natives who are capable of filling responsible positions with credit is a matter that deserves careful consideration. It is neither just nor expedient to subject men of this class to laws and regulations appropriate only to ·tribal or semi-civilised natives, and exemptions from such legislation might well be granted to them far more freely than in the past. It is also worthy of consideration whether further openings might not be found for some of the most capable of these men in somewhat more responsible positions than they at present generally occupy.

§ 2. THE LABOUR QUESTION

It is often stated that the demand for unskilled labour in South Africa is greatly in excess of the supply, and this view was confirmed by the reports of the Transvaal Labour Commission of 1903 and the Native Affairs Commission of 1903–5. The former Commission estimated that in 1903 there were 181,929 labourers at work in the Transvaal, whereas the Commissioners considered that there was then employment for 403,328, and that 196,000 more would be required for the Witwatersrand mines within the next five years. The Native Affairs Commission stated that it saw " every reason to agree with the finding of the Labour Commission," and estimated that at the date of its report (1905) no fewer than 782,000 labourers were required in the various colonies, although not more than 474,472 could reasonably be expected to be at work at any one time, thus leaving an enormous deficiency of 307,528. If these figures could be relied upon as even approximately accurate, the economic position in South Africa would undoubtedly be very serious. But the

estimates made by these Commissions of the labour
requirements of the country were not supported by adequate statistics, and were based to a large extent on
conjectures. The Transvaal Labour Commission pointed
out that exact returns of the labour needs of that
colony for agricultural purposes were not obtainable,
and there is now little doubt that it greatly overestimated the prospective demand for labour on the mines.
It seems probable also that a similar over-estimate was
made by the Native Affairs Commission, for, apart from
the indefinite character of much of the evidence on which
its calculations were based, it does not appear that the
Commissioners attempted to deal fully with two important
factors in the question—the possibilities of economising
labour and of increasing its efficiency. The conclusions of
this Commission with regard to the available supply of
native labour are, however, of remarkable interest for the
evidence they afford of the growing industry of the natives.
In the opinion of the Commissioners, about 50 per cent.
of the male natives between the ages of fifteen and forty,
or about one-tenth of the native population, might on an
average be expected to be at work outside the reserves
and locations at any one time ; and, as the Bantu population of British South Africa (exclusive of labourers
temporarily resident in the country) may be roughly
estimated at 4,500,000, it would appear on this basis that
a continuous force of about 450,000 labourers can be drawn
from the Bantu natives alone. To this number must be
added from 60,000 to 80,000 natives from Mozambique
possibly a small contingent from north of the Zambesi,
and a large number of coloured labourers of " mixed or
other " races, resident in the various colonies. It seems not
unreasonable to estimate that from these additional sources
at least 150,000 labourers should be constantly obtainable,
which would make the total native and coloured labour

force of British South Africa (exclusive of females) about 600,000, or approximately equal to the total white male population of the country. Whether this supply of labour is sufficient, or could be made sufficient, for the unskilled work of the country it is probably quite impossible to say ; but it would seem that a considerable number of farmers and mining companies could employ more natives than they can at present obtain, and the repatriation of the Chinese coolies will undoubtedly cause a large increase in the demand for native labour on the Rand.

How, then, is this apparent deficiency of labour to be met ? The introduction of Asiatics into the country for this purpose is now out of the question. At present there seems to be no prospect of white unskilled labour being employed on any large scale. The latter alternative was rejected by the Transvaal Labour Commission as "condemned by past and present experience as impracticable and impossible"; and, although this experience is of a somewhat limited character, there is no doubt that there is an overwhelming weight of colonial opinion against the employment of white men for unskilled work. This is largely due to a racial instinct or prejudice against the white man doing the same work as the Kafir, but the preference of employers for native labour, on political as well as financial grounds, is probably also an important factor in the question. Possibly the white man and the Kafir cannot with much advantage labour side by side at the same class of work. But it is far from clear that there are no forms of unskilled work in which white men might be employed, apart from natives, with satisfactory results. The two dissenting members of the Transvaal Labour Commission were of opinion "that in many ways the supply of native labour can be supplemented and superseded by white labour"; and this view is strongly supported

by the majority report of the Transvaal Mining Industry
Commission (1907–8). In fact, so convinced were the
Commissioners who signed the latter report that the
employment of white labour on a large scale is both a
wise and practicable policy, that they recommended
stringent measures to promote it. In their opinion, the
employment in the Transvaal mines of natives from
districts outside the limits of British South Africa should
be restricted, and at the end of three years entirely
prohibited ; employers should only be allowed to engage
natives as free labourers without any power of coercing
them ; and active steps should be taken by the Government
to facilitate and encourage the employment of whites.
Startling as the report of the Commission is in its contrast
to the general opinion of South African employers, it
cannot be dismissed lightly. How far white unskilled
labour can be employed with advantage has still to be
proved. The question should at least be considered with
an open mind. In competing with the native the white
labourer must be handicapped by his higher standard of
living and by the exorbitant prices which he often has
to pay for his food, clothing, and lodging. Nevertheless,
in forms of work in which native labour involves heavy
expenses of supervision, it does not seem impossible that
the white man might fully earn his pay. The advocates
of white labour can at least claim that the experiment has
not yet been fairly tried, and that the climatic conditions
of many parts of South Africa do not prohibit it. It
seems hardly likely that native labourers will be superseded by whites in any large numbers, at any rate in the
immediate future, but there is little doubt that the white
man's excessive prejudice against engaging in forms of
work in which natives are employed is often detrimental
to his own interests and to the progress of the country.
The majority of the Mining Industry Commissioners

justly point out that "if the white man is barred from competing industrially with the native, but must make way for him as he advances, then the white man's destiny in this country is fixed; he is doomed to failure."

At present it is more in accord with public sentiment in South Africa to look to increasing the supply and efficiency of native labour as the practical remedy for the difficulties of employers, and much can undoubtedly be done in both directions. Stronger incentives to industry can be supplied by raising the native's standard of living. Obstacles to the free flow of labour can be removed by improving travelling facilities, by providing proper accommodation for natives on the way to their employments, and by abolishing taxes or charges on their passes. Batches of native labourers are now conveyed on the railways at reduced rates, but care is still needed to ensure that they are not exposed to rough or inconsiderate treatment by the railway employees. The food and accommodation provided by many employers are far from satisfactory, and in many cases higher wages might well be paid, for although the rates of pay in the towns and at industrial centres are nominally high, it must be remembered that the native, as was pointed out by the Native Affairs Commission, "has as a rule to pay top prices for his purchases." The general treatment of native labourers by their employers might also often be much more considerate, and, when native overseers are employed, greater care should be taken to see that they do not abuse their authority.

It is also worthy of consideration whether locations could not be established with advantage near some of the industrial centres, where native labourers could be provided with a sufficient amount of land to induce them to reside permanently at such centres with their families. A successful experiment of this kind made by the Indwe Company has already been referred to, and it would often

be in the interests of employers, as well as of the
natives, if some of the more efficient and industrious
labourers could in this way be induced to live within easy
reach of their work. The establishment of locations on
these lines might afford a useful outlet for two increasing
classes of natives for whom provision will have to be made
in the future: the young men who in some congested
districts find it difficult to obtain allotments of tribal
land, and the progressive natives who want better opportunities of improving their position than are generally open
to them under the rule of their chiefs.

It is sometimes urged that the work of collecting native
labour should be undertaken by the various Governments.
The grave objections to this course are forcibly stated
by Sir Godfrey Lagden in a memorandum on Native
Affairs prepared in 1901. "Upon the subject of recruiting,"
he writes, " I have already given expression to the conviction, and desire to reiterate it, that it is, both in the
interests of justice and business, undesirable for magistrates or other officers of Government to be employed to
recruit labour. The labourers should feel certain that, in
case of dispute or grievance, they always have an im-
partial forum to appeal to. If a magistrate becomes a
recruiting agent, his individuality is prejudiced, and all
sense of confidence in him is liable to be lost, not from
any fault of his, but from the fact that he is placed in a
false position towards those he is deputed to advise and
govern." It is, however, clearly the duty of the Government
to exercise a vigilant oversight over the recruiting and
employment of natives, and to protect them from fraud
and ill-treatment. The licensing of labour-agents, the
supervision of contracts by magistrates and pass officers,
the inspection of compounds and places of employment,
the enforcement of rules of hygiene, the prompt redress of
any legitimate grievances, the establishment of labour

bureaux at industrial centres, are all matters that call for, and in a large degree are receiving, the careful attention of the Governments. And magistrates and other Government officials can and do render valuable assistance by encouraging natives to work, and by giving them information as to opportunities of employment. In such ways as these the Governments can do much to lessen the difficulty of obtaining labour ; but it is hardly within their province to collect native labourers for private employers, and it is essential that no duties should be placed upon the magistrates which might prejudice their position in the eyes of the natives.

No justification exists for putting undue pressure on the natives, by taxation or otherwise, to seek employment. As the Native Affairs Commission stated in its report, " Any measure of compulsion is to be deprecated, not only as unjust, but as economically unsound." The Commissioners justly included in this condemnation the widely advocated policy of applying indirect compulsion by means of taxation. " Indirect compulsion," they reported, " in the form of a labour tax, with a remission to workers, has been recommended, but the suggestion appears to the Commission to be open to the same objections as apply to direct compulsion ; in addition to which, any measure of taxation of this kind to be really effective would have to be so high as to be impossible of application." The small labour tax which was imposed under the Glen Grey Act of 1894 has now been repealed, and, except in Rhodesia,[1] no tax of this kind appears to be in force in any part of British South Africa. It may, therefore, be hoped that the policy of

[1] The Rhodesian Government inserted a provision in their agreement with the Fingoes who settled in Rhodesia, that if they failed to give three months' labour, they should be liable to a tax of £3 per annum. Apparently there had been no occasion to enforce this provision. (See Mr. H. J. Taylor's evidence before the Native Affairs Commission.)

imposing taxation for labour purposes has been effectually
discredited. Taxes of this kind are calculated to irritate
the natives and inevitably arouse suspicion as to the
good faith of the Governments : and nothing is more likely
to make labour unpopular than attempts to taint it with
any suggestion of compulsion. Notwithstanding the
protests of magistrates and chiefs, and the recommendations
of Commissions on Native Affairs, one form of compulsory labour is still enforced in Natal. The Governor
as Supreme Chief has power to call out natives to labour
on the roads or public works of the Colony ; and the
magistrates are instructed to require the chiefs to provide
about three thousand men for six months each year for these
purposes. The men who are called out in this way
receive about 20s. a month, with rations and accommodation, but the system is described by the Natal Commission
on Native Affairs as "intensely unpopular," and, in view
of the strong recommendation of that Commission that
some satisfactory substitute should be devised, it is greatly
to be hoped that it will not be continued.

Another important question to which attention was
drawn by the Native Affairs Commission is the
desirability of encouraging the employment of native
women in domestic work. The Commission was of
opinion that a number of men and boys might thus
be released for other and more suitable occupations, and
that the employment of women in this way would tend
to raise the standard of native domestic life. Many native
women are already engaged in laundries and as servants,
but in some parts men and boys are said to be greatly
preferred in the latter capacity. The reluctance to employ
female servants is no doubt mainly due to the girls being
insufficiently trained and cared for, but, with proper safeguards, there seems to be no reason why they should not
be employed more freely. Most native women have

abundant employment at their homes, but some satisfactory form of work is much needed for those who are not thus occupied.

The question of augmenting the supply of native labour has often been considered without due regard to the possibility of increasing its efficiency. Yet it seems not improbable that it is in the latter direction that relief from the present labour difficulties can most profitably be sought. The Natal Commission on Native Affairs described the state of native labour in that colony as " wasteful and uneconomic in the extreme," and urged the introduction, with the co-operation of chiefs and heads of kraals, of " a system of apprenticeship of youths to responsible European employers under proper safeguards as to teaching, food, clothing, housing, etc." Mr. Maurice S. Evans, a member of that Commission, points out that the defective training of native labourers and servants is largely due to the use of " kitchen Kafir " as the medium of communication between them and their employers. In this makeshift for a common language "it is impossible," writes Mr. Evans,[1] " for the employer to correctly express his meaning, and misconception ensues—the waste of time and effort from this source alone is appalling." There is little prospect of removing this difficulty until employers realise the advantages to be gained by teaching the natives English and giving them elementary instruction. At present too many employers are content to express their preference for uneducated natives, and seem indifferent to any efforts either to improve the character of native education or to extend its benefits. So long as these employers are satisfied to rely on untrained employees, to whom they can only give the simplest instructions, so long will the potential labour resources of the country remain

[1] In an article on " The Native Problem in Natal" in the *Empire Review* of February 1907.

imperfectly utilised. On the other hand, employers who have carefully trained their natives have been well rewarded for their trouble ; and it is only by means of such training that labour can be economically applied and progressive methods of agriculture and industry introduced.

The persistence of conservative methods and deeply rooted prejudices still tends to perpetuate the characteristic inefficiency of native labour, but new wants and new standards of living have undoubtedly aroused a healthy and growing spirit of industry among the natives. " The theory that the South African natives are hopelessly indolent may be dismissed as being not in accordance with the facts," was the conclusion at which the Native Affairs Commission arrived after its searching inquiries, and it is fully borne out by the facts and figures which have been summarised in this chapter. The solution of the labour question is being gradually effected by economic and social forces more potent than any measures of compulsion, and with results more radical and far-reaching than those who originally set them in motion might have cared to contemplate. But in this remarkable development of the great latent powers of the native peoples of South Africa, under wise and sympathetic guidance, lies the hope of their future progress and of the peace and prosperity of the country.

CHAPTER II

LAND TENURE

§ 1. INTRODUCTORY

THE natives are primarily agriculturists, and the tribal system under which most of them still live is so interwoven with the possession of land that every development of the land question is of peculiar interest. No great changes have taken place in this respect during the last few years, but much valuable information has been collected by the recent Commissions, and recommendations have been made as to the holding and occupation of land by natives which may have far-reaching effects on their prosperity. Before considering proposals for the future, however, it seems well to give a brief summary showing how the native population of British South Africa is distributed over the land at the present time.

§ 2. CAPE COLONY

The policy of Cape Colony has been gradually to adapt communal land holding to the changing conditions. The aim has been, in conjunction with a just administration of tribal affairs, to prepare the way for individual tenure and local self-government. The lands occupied by natives were on annexation reserved for them, and over a million of the native population now occupy communally lands which have been thus specially set aside. These lands, which include a large portion of the Transkeian Territories,[1]

---

[1] The native population of the Territories is about 850,000.

are, for the most part, divided into wards whose limits have been fixed as far as possible according to the occupation of the various tribes when the land was originally taken over. Each ward is under the control of a headman, who allots, subject to the approval of the magistrate, to each native a plot of garden land, in addition to his site for occupation, retaining, however, a large portion of the land for commonage, over which the natives have communal rights of grazing, etc. A native cannot be removed from his holding without the approval of the Chief Magistrate in the Transkeian Territories, or without the approval of the Government in the Colony proper. No lands have been reserved during the last few years for communal occupation, although applications have been made in cases where the present locations are overcrowded.[1]

There are about 40,000 natives living on private locations. For these private locations (some 1,300 in number) further regulations were provided by the Native Locations Amendment Act (No. 30 of 1899),[2] which enacts that the owner of any land on which a private location is established must take out an annual licence for such location. A private location is defined by section 2 of the Act as meaning " any number of huts or dwellings on any private property, occupied by one or more native male adults, such occupants not being in the *bonâ fide* and continuous employment of the owner or occupier of such land, either as his domestic servants or in or about the farming operations, trade, business, or handicraft, by him carried on upon such land." The

---

[1] Evidence of Mr. E. E. Dower, Secretary for Native Affairs, before the Native Affairs Commission, 1903-5, Report, vol. ii. p. 5.

[2] This Act repealed Act No. 33 of 1892 and sections 2, 3, 4, and 6 of Act No. 37 of 1884, and so much of any other law as might be repugnant to or inconsistent with its provisions. It does not apply to any location under Act No. 5 of 1899, or to any location situate within any municipality or area under the operation of the Village Management Acts, unless a municipality or village management board shall apply its provisions to any such location.

owner has to pay on every such annual licence the sum of £1 per annum for every native male adult (except in respect of certain persons specially exempted by section 11) and the hut tax of 10s. per annum. No licence may authorise more than 40 male adults to be at any time in occupation of a private location, nor may any licence be issued in respect of natives, other than those mentioned in section 11, except upon the certificate of the Civil Commissioner that the consent of the Divisional Council and the Governor to the issuing of such licence has been obtained. Amongst the persons specially exempted by section 11 are " Any native male adults who are *bonâ fide* required for the due working of any private property." This important exemption has proved of great assistance to farmers who require an increased supply of labour at certain seasons of the year, and over one thousand " Labour Tenant Locations " have been established, and appear to give universal satisfaction.[1]   These small locations generally consist of not more than five or six natives and their wives and children, and the number of natives " *bonâ fide* required" is decided by the Inspector of Native Locations.[2] The usual arrangement with the native labour-tenant is for him to work for the farmer during certain periods of the year, his rent being determined by the amount of such labour, and the quantity and quality of the land which he is allowed to cultivate for his own use. In some cases the farmer places certain lands at the disposal of the natives, who do nothing else but work thereon, and then share the profits with him.   Private locations which simply consist of land farmed out to natives, and which

---

[1] Mr. S. H. Roberts, Chief Inspector of Native Locations, reported that "the introduction of section 13 (Labour Tenant Locations) into Act No. 30 of 1899 has to a great extent decreased the difficulty farmers formerly had in obtaining labour for the cultivation of their land. . . ." Cape Colony Blue Book on Native Affairs, 1904, p. 45.

[2] Act No. 30 of 1899, section 13.

may be termed "Squatters' Locations," seem to be unsatisfactory in principle, and are discouraged. Exemption from payment of licence fees is granted in cases where native male adults jointly occupy any private property as registered owners, or who jointly have a *bonâ fide* written lease, but the rent in the case of two such lessees must be £48 or upwards and not less than an additional £12 each for any greater number of lessees.[1] The occupation of private property by a native who is the sole registered owner, or who is the sole lessee paying a rent in cash of not less than £36 per annum under a *bonâ fide* written lease, does not constitute a private location.[2] Complaints are made that bogus agreements are entered into for the purpose of obtaining the benefit of these exemptions.

The owner of any land on which a private location is established has to keep a register of the huts and dwellings, the names and occupations of the native male adults and particulars of the horses, horned cattle, sheep, and goats within the location.[3]

In certain areas where large numbers of natives are engaged in mining or any public or private works the Governor may suspend the operation of the ordinary Location Acts and declare a district to be a proclaimed area subject to the provisions of the Native Labour Locations Act (No. 5 of 1899). Under this Act a register has to be kept of the number of huts and names of the natives and with particulars as to the cattle. Natives have to be furnished with tickets, and unauthorised persons may be ejected. An example of a location of this kind is given by Mr. G. E. Dugmore, the managing director of the Indwe Railway, Collieries, and Land Company, Ltd., who informed this Committee that (in 1902) "the Indwe Company have between 200 and 300 families settled on land adjacent to their mines ; they give each man six acres of land to culti-

[1] Act No. 30 of 1899, section 10.   [2] *Ibid.* section 9.   [3] *Ibid.* section 8.

vate, and grazing for a limited number of live stock, for which a rent of £3 per annum is paid. They sign a contract to work 18 days in each month at current rate of wages (about 2s. per day). This answers well in keeping skilled native labour together ; in actual practice, they do not on an average work more than 15 days a month, and constant supervision is necessary to secure even so much. On the whole, the system works well, and we are extending it. Under the provisions of one of our Acts of Parliament, the Governor may proclaim areas contiguous to mines as areas within which intoxicating liquor shall not be sold to natives. This is a proclaimed area, and all canteens have been closed. A trifling amount of smuggling exists, but we have no trouble among the 1,500 natives we are now employing. I strongly advocate *total prohibition* to natives." In May 1903 Mr. Dugmore again wrote: " On 1st April last the lease of one of our farms fell in. I had 51 allotments surveyed, and within a month all were taken up and more are being applied for. This makes the fifth farm thus utilised, the sixth will be similarly dealt with on 1st January next, when present lease falls in, and other farms will follow as required."

Locations on Crown and private land in the Transkeian Territories are regulated by Proclamations, which in the main follow the Cape legislation.

Large numbers of natives working in towns reside in urban locations, established within municipal areas for residential purposes. It is also provided by the Native Reserve Locations Act (No. 40 of 1902) and the Native Reserve Locations Amendment Act (No. 8 of 1905) that the Governor may by proclamation establish native locations in or near a city, and may prescribe and define the limits of any urban district in which a native reserve location shall have been established and proclaim such urban district (excluding the area of such location) to be an area within which it shall not be lawful for any native to reside, with the exception of (*inter alia*) a native in *bonâ fide* employment as a domestic or farm or other servant and housed on his master's premises, or a native who has been granted special permission to reside outside the location. These locations are subject to stringent sanitary and other regulations; but the standard of comfort is often low and the accommodation inadequate. Referring to the locations at East London, in which about 11,000 natives live, Mr. C. A. Lloyd, the superintendent, stated in his evidence before the Native Affairs Commission that " a site of 40 feet by 40 feet, upon which one hut is allowed to be erected, is obtainable in the municipal locations of East London on payment of a monthly fee of 2s., which covers the cost of water and sanitary expense; an additional charge of 4s. is made in the case of an occupier desiring to accommodate lodgers." [1] In the Ndabeni Location near Capetown, which was started in 1901, the rent is 10s. per month for a lean-to hut and £2 a month for a Government cottage with two rooms.

Outside areas thus set apart for native occupation, there has been no restriction to the acquisition of land by natives in the open market; and a considerable number of natives have purchased land. A few wealthy ones own large amounts, and instances are mentioned of individual natives owning 12,000 and as much as 100,000 acres freehold.[2] "Since my appointment here, a little over three years ago," [3] writes Mr. J. H. O'Connell, the Civil Commissioner, Komgha, in his report for the year 1905, " natives have acquired by purchase title to some 16,500 acres of land in this

---

[1] Report, vol. v. p. 52.
[2] Report of Commissioner for Native Affairs on Acquisition and Tenure of Land by Natives in the Transvaal. Appendix 7 E (a).
[3] Cape Colony Blue Book on Native Affairs, 1905, p. 19.

district." Such property would in most cases be actually occupied by groups of natives under communal tenure. Sometimes natives have combined in the purchase of freehold land and remain as joint owners.

Endeavours have from time to time been made to encourage the development of the principle of individual tenure within tribal areas where the native has progressed sufficiently to avail himself of it with advantage. Under the Glen Grey Act, 1894, the most recent and important attempt in this direction, an allottee of land pays an annual quit-rent of 15s. for a garden allotment of four morgen, and 3s. for every additional morgen above five, and may not alienate or transfer his land without the consent of the Governor, or mortgage or in any way pledge his interest therein.[1] The Glen Grey Act, 1894, has been amended by the Glen Grey Amendment Acts of 1899 and 1905 ;[2] and the provisions relating to the individual holding of land by natives have been extended by proclamation to the Transkeian districts of Butterworth, Nqamakwe, Tsomo and Idutywa. Recent surveys have, as far as possible, proceeded on the principle of allotting to each native the land occupied by him at the time of survey, so as to avoid disturbing him in his cultivation. In describing the methods adopted in making the survey of the Butterworth district, Mr. E. Gilbert Hall, one of the Government land surveyors, stated in his evidence before the Native Affairs Commission that[3] "some natives are found cultivating ground of not more

[1] For particulars as to this Act and the previous experiments in individual land-holding see "The Natives of South Africa" (John Murray), p. 76 et seq.

[2] Amongst other amendments, it may be mentioned that allotments are not to be liable in the future to execution for debt, and that a life interest is reserved to the wife during widowhood on the death of the owner.

[3] Report, vol. ii. p. 930.

than a morgen and a half in extent, others, again, are found
cultivating ten or twelve morgen. They vary considerably,
and they vary in accordance with the quality of the soil.
We find that the natives living on the slopes of the Kei
River, and such-like places, where the soil is very rich,
cultivate very small pieces of ground indeed. Our difficulty
as a Commission was to persuade these men, if possible,
to give up these small pieces and move on to the flats,
where we could give them new ground, four morgen in
extent ; but in the majority of cases they preferred these
little pieces of ground. The result was that, rather than
force them out, we had to survey these pieces of ground,
however small they were, because they preferred them.
The consequence is that some of the titles now being
issued are for ground much less than four morgen in size ;
but I think the average of lots throughout the Butterworth
district works out at about four morgen or slightly over,
because there are, as I say, a large number in excess of
the four morgen." Practically all the surveyed plots in
the Glen Grey district have been taken up, and the
majority of these allotments consist of four morgen, or a
little over eight acres, but some are larger, and most of
the headmen have received thirty morgen. The natives
have only in a very few cases availed themselves of the
provision which enables them to apply for the grant of
a building lot on their giving proof that they are able to
erect a substantial building upon the lot within a reasonable time. They seem to prefer to live scattered all over
the commonage, as they are not supposed to build on their
garden plots. The system of granting individual allotments is working well, and Mr. C. J. Warner, Resident
Magistrate, Nqamakwe, states that[1] "the survey of this
district is proceeding apace, and the natives, who are very
anxious to obtain titles to their allotments, take great

[1] Cape Colony Blue Book on Native Affairs, 1904, p. 123.

interest in the matter. As the system of individual tenure
is extended and better understood, there can be no doubt
it will become more popular, and more districts will apply
to come under it. Natives begin to recognise the fact that
in districts occupied communally land questions become
more acute every year, while applicants for arable lands
steadily increase in numbers. They begin to see that a
system of individual land tenure founded on the Glen Grey
Act places all land matters on a sound footing, and
definitely secures to each person the possession of his
allotment." Mr. Warner writes further, in his report for
the year 1906 : [1] " The detailed survey of this district was
completed last October. A great many individual titles
have been issued, and during the past two years the
natives have been paying the costs of survey of their
allotments." In the district of Butterworth, according to
the report of Mr. W. T. Brownlee, the Resident Magistrate,
the principle of individual tenure has been applied and
has given every satisfaction.[2] Mr. J. P. Cumming, the
Resident Magistrate, Idutywa, reports : [3] " During 1905
the people applied that the survey be extended to this
district. During 1906 the Government authorised the
preliminary survey to be undertaken ; and the surveyor-
in-charge actually began the work, but the Government
gave orders to defer the survey. It is a matter of great
regret that the work, having once been begun, should be
stopped. With natives this is a fatal error to make. It
would have been better not to have started this work at
all." The survey of this district was proceeded with in
1907. Mr. N. O. Thompson, the Resident Magistrate,
Kentani, also reports : [4] " The system of individual tenure
of land has not yet been introduced, but I trust that in
due course this survey of the land will also be extended

[1] Cape Colony Blue Book on Native Affairs, 1906, p. 75.
[2] *Ibid.* 1904, p. 121.   [3] *Ibid.* 1906, p. 75.   [4] *Ibid.*

to the district." The introduction of the system is also desired in the Engcobo District, and elsewhere.

> In the native territories (writes Canon H. R. Wood-rooffe) titles are now being issued in certain districts— those which may be called conquered districts. And this I hold to be a wise policy. Those districts were split up into locations, each of which was in charge of a headman. Many of these headmen use their power for their own profit, and are guilty of continual acts of oppression. The granting of titles will abolish their power, or very materially curtail it. And of course it will tend towards progress, as the sense of security will induce many both to build and to cultivate more carefully than hitherto. I think, however, that some territories or districts which were voluntarily placed under British protection ought to be treated differently from those which I call con- quered districts. The wishes of the people should be consulted and acted upon. And if the issuing of titles is not generally desired, the principle of justice would be infringed were it made compulsory. I refer to Tembuland, Pondoland, and the Baca country.

Complaints are often made that the holding of allot- ments under the Glen Grey Act confers no political franchise, and this no doubt tends in some cases to lessen the desire of the natives for these allotments. But the establishment of local councils for the management of the affairs of each locality, which is one of the new departures made possible under this Act, tends to educate the natives for self-government, and encourages their sense of civic responsibility.

§ 3. NATAL

In *Natal* the conditions of native land tenure are very different from those in Cape Colony; and there is no evidence of a definite policy for the development of the large native agricultural population by improving their methods of tenure or occupation.

In 1864 about 2,200,000 acres in Natal were set apart
for natives and the Natal Native Trust was formed, with
powers to "grant, sell, lease, or otherwise dispose of the
same lands as they should deem fit, for the support, advantage, or well-being" of the natives of the Colony (not only
for those occupying at the time). There are also 127,211
acres in Mission Reserves. The Natal Native Trust, which
was made sole trustee for these grants in 1903,[1] has power
to make transfers of land to natives, provided the purchase-
money is used for improvement of the lands, or for similar purposes. The Trust has also power to charge rent, and under
its regulations a rent of £1 10s. per annum is payable in
respect of every hut or dwelling in a Mission Reserve.

Natives own 67,957 acres in freehold and 33,515 acres
in quit-rent. They have also purchased 215,516 acres of
Crown lands under long terms of payment. In some cases
the purchasers have been individual natives, in others
syndicates of natives; and these lands have frequently
been let to native tenants.[2]

Excluding those natives living in towns or on Crown
lands, only about one-third (265,603) of the natives of Natal
proper live on the lands set apart for them in the Native
Trust or in the Mission Reserves. The other two-thirds
(421,080) live as tenants on land belonging to private and
often absentee white owners, and are liable to ejectment.
On the occupied farms they pay rents varying from £1
to £5 per annum; their landlords often make claims on
their labour when it suits their purposes, the rent paid
varying according to the amount of such demands. On
the unoccupied farms they pay rent, but are usually
free to dispose of their labour. Natives living on Crown
lands pay a rent of £2 per hut per annum.

The following extracts from magisterial reports show the

[1] Act No. 49 of 1903.
[2] The Native Affairs Commission, 1903-5, Report, vol. i. p. 20.

difficulties which have been growing up round the present
land system for many years.

Mr. J. J. Field, the Magistrate for the Mapumulo
Division, reported for the year 1898 [1].

> With the exception of some lands which have been
> set apart and ceded to trustees in trust for foreign
> missions, the division consists of location lands, and is
> inhabited almost entirely by natives, the only Europeans
> being a few storekeepers and missionaries, and others
> connected with mission work. The area of the division
> is officially given as 390 square miles. The native
> population is nearly 35,000 souls, the division being
> the most thickly populated in the Colony, there being
> 21·5 huts and 89 souls to the square mile, Indwedwe
> being next, with a population of about 60 souls
> to the square mile. At present there appears to be
> quite sufficient land for the wants of the natives.
> Natives build their kraals and cultivate their gardens
> where it best suits their liking ; and I fear that fact,
> coupled with their rapid increase, and owing to the
> wasteful manner in which they cultivate the land, that
> in the near future the location lands here will be found
> to be quite inadequate for the requirements of the popu-
> lation. If some official supervision could be exercised
> over the locations, and the natives gradually instructed
> to utilise the land to a greater extent than they do, and
> their kraals could be grouped together more than is
> now the case, the present condition of affairs might
> last for many years to come.

Mr. F. E. Foxon, the Magistrate for the Ixopo Division,
reported for the year 1905 [2]:

> The natives are well off for food, but, owing to their
> constantly being ejected by Europeans who require
> the use of the private farms, and the Crown lands being
> purchased by Europeans, who often eject all the
> native tenants, etc., considerable discontent does exist
> amongst many tribes.

[1] Natal Blue Book on Native Affairs, 1898, B 3.   [2] *Ibid* 1905, p. 1.

Mr. J. L. Knight, the Magistrate for the Alexandra Division, reported for the year 1905 [1]:

> The land question is becoming a very serious matter. Crown lands are gradually being sold, and the new landlords are making the terms of occupation more and more stringent. When natives are unable to meet these their only refuges are the locations, and these are becoming so congested as to have almost reached their limit, at any rate under the present system.

The Natal Native Affairs Commission (1906-7) strongly condemned the conditions that have been allowed to grow up in this way. Not only have strained relations arisen between tenant and landlord owing to the high rents that are exacted, but the chasm between the races has been broadening for years. The attitude of the natives is described as being one of distance and distrust. They feel as if the hand of the Government were against them. Their ability to meet the increasing obligations has been lessened by the growing neglect of proper cultivation, and they take their ideas of the protection of Government from the procedure to enforce the obligations. The policy has been to reduce the size of the tribes and curtail the power of the chiefs. While the collective tribal aims of former times now find no outlet, individual aspirations are expected of them in the direction of personal effort and satisfaction.

According to the terms of the annexation of Zululand and Amatongaland to Natal in 1897, the existing communal land system was to remain unaltered for five years, and then a Commission was to be appointed for the purpose of delimiting sufficient land reserves in the Province of Zululand for native locations. A joint Imperial and Colonial Commission (The Zululand Lands Delimitation Commission) was accordingly appointed in 1902, and issued its report [2] in 1904, setting out the lands to be reserved

---

[1] Natal Blue Book on Native Affairs, 1905, p. 13.

[2] Apparently, this report has not yet been carried into effect.

for native occupation and showing the parts of the country
to be thrown open to European occupation. The Commissioners state that "there can be little doubt that the
effect of the delimitation will not be realised and be brought
home to the natives until European occupation is an
accomplished fact; but, in our opinion, no trouble need
ensue, provided the natives are treated with consideration
and justice." It would seem to be of the utmost importance that ample provision of land should be made for the
overflow of natives from Natal as well as for the native
population of Zululand. In the opinion of the Natal Commission on Native Affairs the salvation of the Colony of
Natal depends on relieving the congestion on the private
lands by finding places for some of the population on
reserves formed in Zululand.

In Natal and Zululand the struggle for the land is the
struggle for life, and the future of the agricultural natives
depends upon a clear opening being made for their development. A suggested agency for improvement is the establishment of communal settlements in locations controlled
by village councils. A form of self-government, and the
issue of conditional titles to secure fixity of tenure and
beneficial occupation in such communities, are advocated as
important steps in gradually detribalising the natives. The
locations in Natal may, under better supervision, be made
to carry more population. Little effort certainly has been
made in the past in this direction.[1] The tenants themselves
may be led with care to leave their wasteful pastoral habits
and make better use of the land under improving methods
of agriculture; some may be encouraged to form a class of
farm labourers, instead of depending on inferior systems of
tenancy. A general policy is advocated of limiting squat-

[1] The Natal Native Affairs Commission, 1906-7, reported that the
full and economical occupation of these locations had been glaringly
neglected. Report, p. 8.

ters to the requirements of labour on the farms and of
drafting ejected farm tenants, of whom there is said to be
an increasing number each year, to Zululand or in one of
the ways suggested above.

§ 4. THE TRANSVAAL

In this Colony 2,120 square miles of land have been set
aside as Government locations for natives. They make no
payments for rent, and enjoy common rights in regard to
water, wood, and grazing. The boundaries of many of
these locations, which are occupied, it is estimated, by
123,309 natives, are not exactly defined, and many tribes
claim that promised grants of locations have not been
made. A Commission was appointed in the year 1905 to
inquire into these matters, and it is hoped that its inquiries
will result in a satisfactory provision of land being made
for the natives.[1]

Natives own 853 square miles of land, nearly all of
which has been purchased by tribal subscription and is
occupied communally. Most of this land is situate in the
Central and Western Transvaal. It had become the
practice in the Transvaal to refuse the transfer of land to
a native, and the Government nominated a trustee, in
whose name such land could be registered. In some
cases, however, the registration was effected in the names
of unofficial Europeans or missionaries. It has recently
been decided by the Supreme Court of the Transvaal (in
the case of *Tsewu* v. *Registrar of Deeds*[2]) that an aboriginal
native of South Africa is entitled to claim transfer in the
Deeds Office of land of which he is the owner.

About one half (438,000) of the natives permanently
resident in the Transvaal live on farms owned by Euro-

[1] Transvaal Native Affairs Department Annual Reports, 1904-5, B 17,
and 1905-6, A 24.
[2] 1905 ; T.S. 130.

peans and companies.[1]   These natives either work unpaid
for the owners (being allowed in return to squat on the
land, with a plot of land for their own cultivation, which
the farmer often ploughs and sows for them) or they pay a
yearly rent of from £1 to £5.   Many of these farms are
more or less uncultivated, and are either situated in unhealthy
areas, where settlement by Europeans is almost impossible,
or are owned by land companies and others, who hold
them for the sake of their prospective value for development for mining and other purposes, and in the meantime
either receive the benefit of the natives' work or the rents
paid by them.   This system of "farming natives" has
become a far-reaching evil.   The usual arrangement
between the *bonâ fide* farmer and the natives whom he
requires for the working of his farm seems to have worked
fairly well in the past.   The law forbidding the settlement
of more than five families on any one farm without the
consent of the Government has been disregarded, and
there are many communities of natives farming unauthorised locations on private land.   There are also a large
number of natives, estimated at 180,427, living as squatters
on open Crown lands, which were formerly their property,
and for whom no definite locations have been laid out.
These natives, from whom a rent of £1 per annum per
cultivator was demanded for the first time in 1904, enjoy
free water and grazing rights.   In his annual report for
the year 1905–6, Mr. W. A. King, the Sub-Native Commissioner, Potgietersrust, states :

> The collection of Crown rents must be considered
> satisfactory in view of the enormous difficulties
> encountered by the collector in these parts, where the
> majority of the Crown lands are still unsurveyed, and
> in most cases difficult of access.[2]

[1] The Native Affairs Commission, 1903-5, Report, vol. i. p. 23.
[2] Transvaal Native Affairs Department Annual Report, 1905-6, B 48.

Locations have been established in many places for natives working in towns or mines. In the year 1906 the native location in Johannesburg was removed by the Town Council to the outskirts of the municipality. In this new location native tenants are able to acquire individual holdings under leases extending over a period of 33 years. Plots of land are let to natives at a small rental for them to build houses on. Buildings erected by the municipality are let at a reasonable monthly rental. Sir Godfrey Lagden reported as to this location as follows: "I rejoice to think that the new native location at Klipspruit, near Johannesburg, promises to be a model. The municipality has spared neither efforts nor expense to make it so." It is hoped that similar locations, which should attract a good class of natives, may be formed near other towns.

§ 5. SWAZILAND

This territory has been placed recently under the direct control of the High Commissioner, and portions of the country have been reserved exclusively for the use and occupation of the natives.

§ 6. ORANGE RIVER COLONY

In *the Orange River Colony* there are two reserves at Witzies Hoek and Moroka, occupied on communal tenure by 17,000 natives. When Paulus Mopeli, a Mosuto chief, desired in 1867 to come under the Orange Free State Government, an ordinance was passed defining the conditions under which the tribe should occupy his location at Witzies Hoek. The land was vested in the Government; no power to alienate was granted to the natives, and no rent imposed. A Commandant was appointed, who allotted the land in the location, which became practically a location under a magistrate, with the chief as his medium of authority. The location remains as at first beaconed off, with the exception of a piece of land granted to the Dutch Reformed Church. On the death of Paulus Mopeli further regulations were made in 1898. In the year 1884 the territory of Sepinari Moroka was annexed by President Brand, who guaranteed existing rights. Before annexation the chief had agreed to grant separate titles to members of his family and others, including a few whites. The Government gave effect to these arrangements, the rights of the Barolongs then squatting on these lands being respected. To protect the natives from parting with their rights, the Volksraad resolved shortly afterwards that these lands could only be sold with the approval of the Volksraad, a pre-emptive right of purchase being reserved by the Government, and that alienation should not be allowed for fifteen years. A large strip of this country has, however, passed into private hands, and the remainder is now Government property. Most of the latter portion has been set apart as locations, which natives occupy under communal tenure, and an Act of the Legislature would probably be required to remove them. The resident magistrate controls the locations, but there is no paramount chief, and the allotment of land appears to be arranged by each separate kraal.

Natives are forbidden to purchase or lease land elsewhere in the Orange River Colony. The great mass of the native population live in small groups on private farms, and 195,494 were so distributed at the date of the Native Affairs Commission Report. Not more than five families of natives[1] are permitted on one farm, unless

---

[1] Law No. 4 of 1895. Single natives who are hired by the owner, lessee, or white occupier, and native families engaged for temporary work such as dam-making, well-digging, etc., do not come within this restriction.

special permission is granted by the landrost of the district; but in any case the number may not exceed fifteen families, and for each family above ten the owner has to pay a tax of £5 per annum. Only two families of natives are allowed to be kept on farms not occupied by a white person. The landrost has to keep a register of the permits granted by him, and the reasons in each case.

Municipalities and village management boards have powers conferred on them for establishing locations within their boundaries for the residence of coloured people. A large location has been established at Bloemfontein for natives working in the town. This location, in which over 18,000 natives reside, is controlled by the municipality. The regulations forbid any natives living there without a permit, but it has been difficult to exclude trespassers. Plots of land, measuring 50 feet by 50 feet, are granted to the natives for them to build houses on. A few houses have been built at a cost of from £250 to £300, but most of them are constructed of raw brick and straw, with an iron roof, at a cost of £9 to £12, and usually consist of only two rooms. Nearly all the natives at Bloemfontein, with the exception of those for whom accommodation is provided by employers on their premises, reside in this location.

§ 7. THE BECHUANALAND PROTECTORATE

In *the Bechuanaland Protectorate* 127,630 square miles of land are set aside for the native population, and are held communally. In good seasons the natives grow more grain than they require for themselves, and are able to sell the surplus; but the land is, for the most part, waterless and unproductive. It only carries a population of ·78 to the square mile, and in bad seasons grain has to be bought.

Land for personal occupation is allotted by the chiefs, and the tribe has common grazing rights, but no green wood is allowed to be cut. A few farms are owned by natives.

§ 8. BASUTOLAND

In *Basutoland* the whole of the land is reserved for the natives, who occupy it under tribal tenure, grazing being in common, and the allotment of arable plots resting with the native chiefs. Nearly the whole of the available arable land is under cultivation. The purchase of land by whites within this territory is not permitted, and it is hoped that Basutoland will continue to be a country reserved for native occupation.

§ 9. SOUTHERN RHODESIA

In *Southern Rhodesia* 38,871 square miles of land are set aside for native reserves. The natives thereon, numbering 264,618, pay poll-tax but no rent, and enjoy water, wood, and grazing rights in common. The garden plots in these reserves are allotted by the native chiefs. Large numbers of natives, estimated at 151,503, live on unreserved and unalienated lands of the Chartered Company, and are liable to be removed to reserves without compensation or to be charged rent. About 62,727 natives live in private locations, which have been established on farms under a Proclamation of October 14, 1896, and they usually pay a yearly rent of £1 per hut in money or labour. Tenancy agreements between landlord and tenant are common. These agreements are made with the approval of the Native Commissioner and registered, the terms being explained to the native. The usual rent is £1 per hut per annum, but sometimes there is a labour agreement for three months'

work. The native appears, however, to prefer to pay rent.
In his report for the year 1906–7, the Chief Native Commissioner, Matabeleland, states :[1] " Agreements between
owners of farms and natives occupying lands thereon are
becoming more general, but in many instances natives
prefer moving on to the reserves to binding themselves to
any definite contract. In a few instances the Matabele
have acquired plots of land from Europeans, and inquiries
have elicited the fact that the tendency in this direction is
likely to increase. Five Fingoes obtained final title to their
allotments, pending the completion of the survey thereof.
These titles are modelled upon the provisions of the ' Glen
Grey Act.'"

§ 10. SUMMARY

It would seem that the communal system of land tenure
will for some considerable time be the one best adapted
to the requirements of the great mass of the native
population. The native is accustomed to its restraints,
and no sudden breaking down of it should be attempted.
At the present time about 2,500,000 natives, more than
one half of the entire native population of British South
Africa, occupy communally 220,470 square miles of land,[2]
which have been reserved for them. It appears, however,
that the parcelling out of the land by the headmen and
chiefs is not always satisfactory. There is often no proper
system of control, and disputes about land are frequent.
The cultivation of the land does not, moreover, produce the
best results, and land is often abandoned after a few years
and fresh land cultivated. Mr. D. Strachan stated before
the Native Affairs Commission that if the natives in the

[1] British South Africa Company's Report, 1906-7, p. 39.
[2] 127,630 square miles of this land are situated in the Bechuanaland
Protectorate, where the land is, as has been seen, for the most part, only
capable of supporting a sparse population.

Transkei were allowed to go on in their present wasteful way in the handling of land, with want of method and want of economy, about ten years would see the end of it, and the question would become very difficult to tackle. Mr. F. Kuys, Resident Magistrate, Taungs, reports for the year 1906 [1]:

> It seems a great pity that the natives make hardly any use (from an agricultural point of view) of the Hartz and Dry Hartz valleys, which are most fertile, and with very little trouble and expense could be watered all the year round. The soil in these valleys is magnificent, and I should say would grow practically everything. At present they still only cultivate inferior mealies, kafir corn, millet (a kind of bean), and an insipid sort of water melon. The beneficial effects of improvements in cultivation they cannot, or will not, recognise, and hence they have made no material advance during the century or more that they have been in contact with civilisation. The reserve is fairly well stocked with cattle of a sort, and, on the whole, these are in good condition now, but, on the other hand, small stock are scarce and poor. This latter, I imagine, may be accounted for by the fact that no attempt is made by the Batlapin to improve the breed he possesses: quantity, and not quality, being his ruling aim. The chief of Manthe, Kgantlapane, preserves to some extent the wood left in his portion of the reserve, but, in Molala's part there is almost nothing left, and even that useful and valuable bush, the " vaalbosch," has been almost entirely eradicated.

The same complaints of inefficient or deteriorating methods of agriculture are heard from Natal, the Transvaal, and elsewhere. Sir Alfred E. Pease, formerly Resident Magistrate for the Barberton District, Transvaal, writes: " Cultivation round native kraals is primitive and wasteful. Valuable timber in the creeks is burnt and destroyed in order to obtain for a short period patches of rich virgin soil

[1] Cape Colony Blue Book on Native Affairs, 1906, p 33.

—quickly abandoned. Where natives are allowed to destroy forest trees they should be compelled to afforest and plant, under supervision of the Forest Department, with free labour, a double or treble area."

Every encouragement should be given to all movements, such as the Glen Grey Act, directed to increasing the individual holding of land by the native where he desires to have it and is able to benefit by it. The gradual extension of this system will give to the native an incentive to work, increase his self-respect, and tend to lessen the power of the chiefs. It will, moreover, tend to a better and less wasteful cultivation of the land than exists where he feels his tenure more or less insecure. The Native Affairs Commission considered that [1] where individual tenure could with advantage be granted in respect of location and reserve land now held by natives under the communal system, it should be granted, subject to the payment of an annual rent, and to liability to forfeiture in case of rebellion, failure to occupy beneficially, or to pay any rent or tax, or a second conviction for stock-theft. All rights to minerals and precious stones should be reserved ; also a right of resumption for public purposes, subject to compensation in land or otherwise. The size of each holding might well be determined by present occupation and quality of land, with a limit, in the absence of special circumstances, of approximately four morgen (8·4 acres). For a long time, in all ordinary cases, mortgaging or pledging must be forbidden, and alienation or transfer only allowed with the sanction of Government. Commonage will have to be set apart, subject, with the holdings, to such duties and regulations as may be established with regard thereto. Three of the Commissioners, Colonel Stanford, Mr. Sloley, and Captain Quayle Dickson, reported, however, as follows:

[1] The Native Affairs Commission 1903–5 Report, vol. i. p. 30.

Natives in the occupation of reserves which have descended to them from their forefathers, or which for other good reasons have been set aside for their permanent use by any Government, have a just claim to a greater fixity of tenure than is implied in the occupation and conditions approved by the majority of the Commission, and more particularly so in respect of those tribes which by voluntary submission to our Government have been received into its protection upon the understanding that, save for rebellion, their land should not be taken from them. They [these Commissioners] are in favour of the principle embodied in the Glen Grey Act, by which perpetual quit-rent title is granted to each individual holder of land upon the subdivision of any location or reserve. Less than this would not, in their opinion, afford an adequate sense of security to natives whose advance in civilised ideas is indicated by their readiness to abandon their long-cherished tribal system of occupation of land ; nor do they think it would be a just recognition of existing rights.

The whole question of the reservation of land for natives requires careful consideration. It would probably be well, as recommended by the Native Affairs Commission, that the land set apart, or to be set apart, for native occupation should be defined by legislative enactment, and that this should be done with a view to making a final provision for the native population. The Commission were, however, of opinion that in setting apart any land, the Crown should reserve all minerals and precious stones, also the right to remove the occupier and to re-enter in case of rebellion and the power to apply regulations.

Of their other recommendations, the one most open to question is that in which they advise that, in order to prevent conflict with European owners, purchase of land by, or leasing of land to, natives should in future be limited to certain areas defined by legislative enactment. The adoption of such a course was dissented from by the Natal delegates and Colonel Stanford, and it would seem to introduce a curtailment of privileges hitherto enjoyed in our Colonies. It was Colonel Stanford's opinion that only in the event of its leading to the extension of the tribal system beyond the reserves or locations would the right of native purchase be contrary to the best interests of both races, and similar views are expressed by some of the Committee's correspondents. " While agreeing," writes Mr. G. E. Dugmore, " with first part of Commission's report in regard to non-advisability of compulsory measures of subdivision, I agree with Colonel Stanford's view, and would not limit the right of the native as a British subject to purchase land wherever he chose, provided it was not for the extension of tribal system. If a native buys a farm among Europeans, he should farm it on European lines, and not establish a location for natives thereon, which would inevitably lead to trouble with his European neighbours, for, unfortunately, experience teaches that sheep-stealing invariably follows." Another of the Committee's correspondents, Mr. John Hemming, for many years Civil Commissioner for the Albany Division in Cape Colony, writes, that, in the Cape Colony,

> there is no restriction to the acquisition of land by natives, and, in my opinion, very justly so. It must not be lost sight of that all land held by Europeans in Africa has been acquired by conquest or diplomacy, and that the aboriginal natives have been ousted by the white man ; that being so, I cannot see any reason that can be advanced why the native should not be allowed to buy back what he has lost ; in my opinion, he should be encouraged to do so where he has the means at his disposal.
> Where a native by his thrift and industry has acquired sufficient money to buy land, why should he be restricted from doing so ? He is a better citizen than the thriftless European who lives from hand to mouth and makes no effort to better his circumstances. I know many natives who have commenced from nothing but their own labour on farms, who are now

worth a great deal of property, well stocked with cattle, sheep, and goats, and who cultivate largely and with success. These men started as young men to work for a European farmer at a remuneration of something like ten or twelve sheep or goats, or an old mare or cow per annum, with their keep, and have gradually, by saving, industry, and trading in live-stock, gone on increasing their means until they had sufficient to buy land. One man, a Fingoe, whom I know, brought £1,600 in gold to me when I was in office many years ago, to count for him, and I saw him hand it over in payment for a farm ; another [as his attorney informed a Commission of which Mr. Hemming was chairman] was worth from £16,000 to £20,000 in land and live-stock. Such men as these and their families have always been peaceful, law-abiding, hard-working citizens, of great assistance to us in native wars, and there can be no reason against their becoming landed proprietors ; on the contrary, they should have every encouragement, and there can be no fear of their behaviour as peaceful citizens now that the power of chieftainship is completely broken.

But it is not with the natives of the Cape Colony that we need be so much concerned, except in the case of future settlements in the Transkeian territories when these come to be made, and then legislation should be carefully watched lest endeavours be made to deprive deserving natives of the privilege of ac-quiring title to land.

In the Transvaal strong efforts are being made to restrict the acquisition of land by natives ; but I can see neither justice nor reason in such a measure. If the native, by his education, honesty, thrift, and industry, has got the means to buy land, even in the Transvaal, why should he not be allowed to do so, under conditions such as reserving to the Government the right to minerals, precious stones, etc., and inserting clauses in his title that the land would be liable to forfeiture in case of rebellion or repeated conviction of theft, or some such crime as would make him an undesirable person to hold land and a nuisance to his neighbours ?

The natives are already pretty tightly " squeezed " in the matter of land in South Africa, and it is time this " squeezing " process came to an end : they must have somewhere to live.   What would we do in this country without them? Where could we obtain a supply of labour without them ?   They are a source of revenue to the country ; they are large consumers of British imports, and if settled on the land are good producers and farmers, paying the same taxes as the Europeans. . . .

In my opinion, there should be large reserves for purely native occupation in each Colony, and within these no encroachment by Europeans should be allowed.   This would render both Europeans and natives happier and better neighbours, and help to do away with the " land hunger " of many people. . . .

It should be noted that in the Transkei, and in other native areas in Cape Colony, Europeans who have obtained the consent of the Government may occupy trading sites, and that Europeans may buy plots in townships which are laid out round magistracies.   Traders are also admitted in other colonies and possessions, but they may not acquire any real right to the land they occupy.   On the other hand, it would appear that if the right of the native be unrestricted, the amount of land in native occupation will probably become greatly extended.   Much irritation would also be occasioned by natives settling in the midst of a white community.   It would seem, therefore, desirable that at any rate certain portions of urban districts should be reserved exclusively for occupation by the white population.   The application of the principle on a large scale seems, however, to be one to which grave exception may be taken.

It is impossible to deal fully here with the many aspects of the land question, but "squatting" and contracts of tenancy seem to require special attention.   The indiscriminate squatting of natives on private and Crown lands has led to many evils, such as absentee landlordism, insecurity of tenure on the part of the natives, and lack of proper control ; it does not encourage the native to go forth to work.   It would seem desirable that legislation on the lines of the Cape Native Locations Amendment Act (No.

30 of 1899) should be introduced in the Transvaal and elsewhere to regulate such occupation, and that its main principles should be applied to natives on Crown lands other than native reserves or locations. The distribution of native families in groups or at centres according to the needs of the land forms a sound basis of policy and affords a fair standard of limitation of squatting. It must prove an advantage to the country to lessen the cost of transport and the dangers incident to labour procured from afar, by more and more securing for each district a resident labouring population according to its needs. It appears that natives are often prevented by the terms of their contracts of tenancy from leaving farms at seasons of the year when their labour is not required, to seek work elsewhere. This not only obstructs the labour supply but closes the door to the advancement of the native. Tenancy agreements with the native are, moreover, usually only verbal, and it would appear that, at any rate where these agreements exceed one year, they should be in writing and attested, so that the terms may be clearly defined and understood.

The condition of the natives differs in each colony or possession. This is in some degree brought about by, and reflects, the widely diverse treatment to which they have been subjected ; but there are certain facts relating to their respective circumstances and distribution which must adversely affect the immediate adoption of any uniform policy. In Cape Colony the natives are placed geographically very favourably from the point of view of administration. The native population is thinnest near the centres of white settlement, the mass of the population occupying outlying territory which it has been easy to set aside as reserved for them. As is natural, the native within easiest reach of contact with Europeans has been most affected, perhaps by the very violence of the contact, and has advanced farther in the direction of understanding European ways. Experiments in individual responsibility, such as the Glen Grey Act, have been applied to the nearest districts beyond the Kei River, and there is every appearance that the continuance of such a careful and liberal policy will result in the extension, however gradual, of civilisation and improved methods of land occupation throughout the remoter native reserves. In Natal, on the other hand, large blocks of land reserved for, or occupied by, native tribes are found in close proximity to the towns and cutting off parts of the white population from others. The importance of friendly relations between native and white colonists is thus enormously enhanced. This was abundantly illustrated during the native rising in Natal of 1906. It is difficult in these circumstances to understand why more has not been done in this colony for the development of native civilisation or for the improvement of their condition. For years the reports of Natal magistrates have acknowledged a want of trust and confidence in many of their districts ; the despatches of the Governor of the Colony during the rising and the report of the Natal Native Affairs Commission 1906–7 give very definite evidence of the alienation of native feeling. The conclusion is inevitable that in Natal the native question will have to be taken up very far back on the road along which Cape Colony has been for some time travelling.

The effect of past treatment of natives in the Transvaal and Orange River Colony is that the tribal units have been far more broken up, and a large proportion of the native population is in small scattered groups.

The mines will no doubt continue to draw their supplies of labour from the Portuguese Territories and from the Native Territories, such as Basutoland and the Transkei, and from the larger native settlements in the reserves in the Transvaal and elsewhere; but even for them the policy has been advocated of encouraging permanent migration to the labour centres and the establishment within easy reach of them of locations or native townships under whatever form of organisation may ultimately prove to be the most convenient and beneficial.

The interests of the whites would thus appear to be identical throughout South Africa. Besides the need for a certain number of labourers to help in the manifold employments of town and port life, the main thought of the European is how he shall obtain a continuous supply of labour for his mines and his farms. This great and crying need has often made him overlook the importance to the rest of South Africa (and the great part that might be played thereby in building up her prosperity) of a really efficient substratum of native agricultural population. Whatever the numbers streaming out to work, the majority will remain occupied with, if not dependent on, their land. The aim should be for the native to become less a pastoral peasant and more an agricultural one; and all movements in this direction, such as facilitating his obtaining the necessary implements of husbandry, should be encouraged.

If the natives, even in unprogressive districts, could be taught to produce more than sufficient for their needs, as that surplus grew they would more and more help to reduce the cost of the necessaries of life to a reasonable and customary price, and they would also take more and more manufactured articles in exchange. It is obvious that this cannot be brought about in a day; it is equally obvious that the natives will not develop in this direction even, without continuous and judicious efforts on the part of the white population.

CHAPTER III

TAXATION

THE practice of raising revenue from the native by means of a tax on his huts has long been established in Cape Colony and elsewhere. Although the tendency in recent years has been to substitute a poll-tax, the old system remains in Cape Colony, Natal, Basutoland, the Bechuanaland Protectorate, and North-Eastern Rhodesia. One of the main differences in the incidence of hut- and poll-tax is that the latter becomes payable at an earlier age than that at which it is customary for a native to have a hut of his own,[1] though contributions towards the hut-tax are often made by the younger natives to the kraal head. As each wife has usually a separate hut, a hut-tax has the effect of taxing the native more heavily if he has more than one wife. This principle has been continued in the Transvaal and Southern and North-Western Rhodesia (where hut-tax has been superseded by poll-tax) by the levying of a special tax in respect of additional wives.

These taxes, particulars of which are given in the statement on the next page, bring in a sum of over £1,000,000 annually.

The Transvaal poll-tax of £2 was imposed by the Native Tax Ordinance, 1902, on every adult male

---

[1] In order to avoid the difficult task of ascertaining the exact age of a native it is merely enacted in the Transvaal and Rhodesia that poll-tax shall be paid by *every adult male native*, and it is left to the discretion of the tax-collector to decide when a native becomes liable.

STATEMENT GIVING PARTICULARS OF HUT- AND POLL-TAXES, AND SHOWING AMOUNTS COLLECTED

Name of Colony or Possession.	Form and Amount of Taxation.	Year.	Amount Collected. £ s. d.
Cape Colony	Hut-tax 10s. per annum for each hut occupied by a native either on a location situated on Crown land or on a "private location," as defined by Act No. 30 of 1899, or on an allotment of tribal land	1907	106,245 18 0[1]
Natal (including Zululand)	Hut-tax 14s. per annum and poll-tax £1 per male of 18 years or upwards, who does not pay hut-tax, per annum	1907, Hut-tax 1907, Poll-tax	180,975 15 0[2] 53,994 10 0[3]
Basutoland	Hut-tax £1 per annum	1906-7	64,870 0 0[4]
Bechuanaland Protectorate	Hut-tax £1 per annum and poll-tax of 5s. per male of full age, not occupying a separate hut, per annum	1906-7	11,606 0 0[4]
Transvaal (including Swaziland)	Poll-tax £2 per male adult per annum, and further tax of £2 per annum if native has more than one wife. The poll-tax of £2 is reduced to £1 in the case of agricultural labourers and municipal location residents	1906-7	334,016 18 0[5]
Orange River Colony	Poll-tax £1 per male between ages of 18 and 60 years per annum.	1906-7	46,229 18 6[6]
Southern Rhodesia	Poll-tax £1 per male adult per annum, and further tax of 10s. per annum for each additional wife.	1906-7	190,958 3 10[7]
North-Western Rhodesia	Poll-tax not exceeding £1 per male of 18 years or upwards per annum, and further tax of 10s. per annum for each additional wife	1906-7	38,294 2 6[7]
North-Eastern Rhodesia	Hut-tax 3s. per male adult per annum	1906-7	15,625 19 0[7]
		Total .	1,041,827 4 10

[1] Cape Blue Book on Native Affairs, 1907, pp. 48, 49, and 52.
[2] Natal Blue Book on Native Affairs, 1907, p. 114. The respective amounts of these taxes collected in Natal and Zululand were as follows: Natal: Hut-tax, £132,429; Poll-tax, £49,637 10s. Zululand: Hut-tax, £48,546 15s.; Poll-tax, £4,267.
[3] Colonial Reports, Basutoland, 1906-7, p. 8.
[4] Colonial Reports, Bechuanaland Protectorate, 1906-7, p. 4. The amount of £11,606 represents the proceeds of the former hut-tax of 10s. per annum; the tax is now £1 per annum.
[5] Finance Accounts of the Transvaal for the Financial Year 1906-7, pp. 6 and 46. The respective amounts of poll-tax collected in the Transvaal and Swaziland were as follows: Transvaal £310,635 18s.; Swaziland £23,381.
[6] Orange River Colony, Colonial Treasurer's Annual Accounts, 1906-7, p. 2.
[7] British South Africa Company's Report, 1906-7, p. 79.

aboriginal native domiciled in the Transvaal. The same Ordinance enacted that if a native had more than one wife, he should pay £2 per annum for each additional wife. These taxes, designed to consolidate the various taxes payable by natives under the late South African Republic, proved too burdensome, and by the Native Tax Amendment Ordinance, 1906, a tax of £2 per annum, if a native had more than one wife, was substituted for the additional wife-tax imposed in 1902. By the same Ordinance the poll-tax of £2 was reduced to £1 in the case of natives who are *bonâ fide* farm labourers and have worked continuously for a certain period, and in the case of natives residing by permission and working within municipal areas and paying municipal taxes. This reduction in the poll-tax was made with the object of encouraging labour.

In the Orange River Colony the poll-tax was increased from 10s. to £1 by the Poll-Tax Consolidation Ordinance, 1904. This tax is imposed on each coloured person of the male sex between the ages of eighteen and sixty years domiciled in the Colony.[1] In Basutoland the hut-tax was raised from 10s. to £1 in the year 1899–1900. In Southern Rhodesia a poll-tax of £1 was imposed in 1904, instead of a former hut-tax of 10s. A further tax was at the same time imposed of 10s. for each wife beyond the first.[2] In North-Western Rhodesia, by Proclamation No. 16 of 1905, which repealed the then existing hut-tax, every male native of 18 years or upwards has to pay such sum, not exceeding £1, as may from time to time be specified by the

[1] The Ordinance mentions certain classes of persons (including persons who have personally resided in the Colony during the whole period for which the tax is payable) who are to be treated as domiciled in the Colony for the purposes of the Act. Certain persons residing on recognised public diggings and persons having rights to land in the Colony and liable to pay quit-rent are exempted from payment of the tax.

[2] Southern Rhodesia Ordinance No. 21 of 1904, section 4.

Administrator, with the approval of the High Commissioner, and, if such native has more than one wife, a further tax of 10s. in respect of each additional wife. In North-Eastern Rhodesia by the Hut-Tax Regulations, 1900, every male native has to pay a hut-tax of 3s., which may be raised to 5s. ,by the Administrator with the consent of the High Commissioner. The Ndola and Loangwa districts, formerly a portion of North-Eastern Rhodesia Territory, were taken over by the North-Western Rhodesia Administration under the High Commissioner's Notice No. 33 of 1905, and the existing tax of 3s. was raised to 5s.

In the Bechuanaland Protectorate the hut-tax has been increased from 10s. to £1 by Proclamation No. 1 of 1907. Referring to this increase of taxation, Mr. Barry May, the Government Secretary for the Bechuanaland Protectorate, states in his report for the year 1906-7 [1] : "Prior to the issue of the Proclamation, the Resident Commissioner visited each of the paramount chiefs (excepting Mathibi in Ngamiland), and explained to them and their people assembled in ' kgotla ' the intentions of the Government in the matter. The news, although naturally not of a character calculated to please, was everywhere received without any manifestations of serious objection. The natives evidently feel that they have been fortunate in only having had to pay 10s. in the past, and are prepared with cheerful resignation to pay the larger sum in future."

Taxation by means of a hut- or poll-tax has become much heavier during recent years in Natal, Basutoland, the Orange River Colony, Rhodesia, and the Bechuanaland Protectorate. The consolidated tax of £2 per annum in the Transvaal appears onerous, and the collection of taxes in that country is more strictly enforced than formerly.

[1] Colonial Reports, Bechuanaland Protectorate, 1906-7, p. 9.

In Cape Colony hut-tax is not chargeable in respect of any occupant of a native location so old or chronically infirm as to be incapable of working.[1] In most of the other colonies and possessions there are various exemptions from payment of the hut- or poll-tax.

It will be seen that these taxes vary considerably in amount. The native is well aware of the differences, but he fails to understand the reason of them. There is a strong consensus of opinion that a more uniform system, possibly with some local graduations, should be adopted throughout the country. In his evidence before the Native Affairs Commission, Sir C. J. R. Saunders, the Chief Magistrate and Civil Commissioner of Zululand, gave as his reasons for thinking such a system desirable that the natives [2] "going about as they do now, working and coming in contact with people from other parts, go back with all sorts of stories that one people are ruled one way, and another in another. They think they should have one system of laws to apply to the whole." Frequent complaints are also made by farmers and others that where taxation is lighter in an adjoining territory natives stray across the border.

The native also contributes largely to the revenue through the customs duties which are levied on goods used and food consumed by him. It is extremely difficult to ascertain at all accurately the amounts paid individually by the natives. Sufficient data cannot be obtained for the purpose. But " an estimate of 2s. per head per annum as the average amount contributed by all the natives throughout British South Africa in indirect taxation appears to be a fair one." [3] On this basis, the amount annually received in this way from natives is nearly

---

[1] Act No. 30 of 1899, section 24.
[2] The Native Affairs Commission, 1903-5, Report, vol. iii. p. 768.
[3] *Ibid.* vol. i. p. 86.

£500,000. This sum, of course, increases year by year with the purchasing power of the native, as he acquires education and becomes more civilised.

How important a consumer he is becoming can be seen from the fact that the following articles, on most of which customs duties had been paid, were imported into Basutoland during the year ending June 30, 1907, [1] viz. :

Articles, etc.	Value.
Animals : horses, cattle, sheep, etc.	£2,567
Apparel, slops, etc.	15,200
Bags of all sorts	7,668
Beads of all sorts	1,069
Cotton piece-goods	12,871
Cotton manufactures	22,146
Food and drink, articles of	23,800
Haberdashery and millinery	17,581
Hardware and cutlery, fencing material, etc. . .	8,473
Hats and caps	1,176
Implements (agricultural)	3,940
Leather and leather manufactures (including boots and shoes and saddlery)	14,485
Soap of all kinds	3,696
Wood, manufactured and unmanufactured . .	4,162
Woollen manufactures (including blankets and shawls)	69,790
All other articles of merchandise	33,729
Total	£242,353

The following statement by Mr. A. S. Leary, the Resident Magistrate for the District of Mount Ayliff in the Transkeian Territories, in his report for the year 1905, gives valuable information as to the trade with natives in that district, and shows the rate of customs duty paid on the various articles imported [2] :

[1] Colonial Reports, Basutoland, 1906-7, p. 10. The above figures include importations of South African produce from other territories amounting to £29,827.

[2] Cape Colony Blue Book on Native Affairs, 1905, p. 48.

"The ordinary native," he writes, "contributes to the revenue by indirect taxation as follows":

Native Traders' Wares. Articles.	Proportion to Total Business.	Rate of Customs Paid by Trader on Article.
Blankets	25 per cent.	} 20 per cent.
Shawls	10 ,,	
Beads	5 ,,	50 ,,
Groceries	5 ,,	
Hoes, etc.	1 ,,	} 7½ ,,
Clothing	30 ,,	
Hardware, various . . .	24 ,,	

In addition to the hut- and poll-taxes and the customs duties, the most important native taxes are fees on passes and for trading and other licences, and dog-tax. Large sums are also received for fines and fees of court. These charges are not uniform in character throughout British South Africa, and where some or all of them are imposed, they vary considerably in amount. They form a large contribution to the revenue of the country. In Natal and Zululand, during the year 1907, the following amounts were received from these sources[1]:

	NATAL.			ZULULAND.		
	£	s.	d.	£	s.	d.
Dog-tax	15,345	5	0	4,303	14	0
Pass fees (including fees under Act No. 49 of 1901) . . .	3,539	9	0	436	19	0
Fees on medical licences . .	2,799	0	0	702	12	6
Fines and fees of court . .	23,108	15	9	3,393	13	6
Fees on Native Christian marriages	432	0	0	71	0	0

[1] Natal Blue Book on Native Affairs, 1907, p. 114.

During the year ending June 30, 1907, the sum of
£3,948 4s. 9d. was received for licence fees in Basutoland,
and the following licences were issued,[1] viz. :

General trader	168
Hawkers (paid)	405
„ (free)	203
Mill licence	1
Labour agents	298

The statement on the next page, which is an extract
from the Annual Report of the Native Affairs Department
for the year ending June 30, 1906, gives particulars
of the laws in force in the Transvaal as to passes for
natives, and the estimated revenue derived therefrom.[2]

By the Registration and Control of Dogs Act, 1907,
a tax of £5 per annum was imposed in the Transvaal
for a Kafir hunting-dog or dog of a similar kind, and
a tax of 10s. per annum in respect of any other kind
of dog.

The natives also pay, in many municipal and other
districts, rates for local purposes. The principle of their
participating in their own local government, including
the levying of rates, has been successfully introduced in
the district of Glen Grey and in a great part of the
Transkeian Territories.[3] To show how largely these
powers of rating have been used, it may be mentioned
that during the year 1907 the Transkeian Territories
General Council received from the proceeds of its general
rate £46,754 10s., the main items of expenditure of the
Council for that period being £16,428 4s. 8d. on education, and £12,690 3s. 11d. on roads.[4] In Crown locations

[1] Colonial Reports, Basutoland, 1906-7, p. 10.
[2] The amounts received in Natal and elsewhere, where pass fees are
mposed, are comparatively insignificant.
[3] See Chapter IV.
[4] Cape Colony Blue Book on Native Affairs, 1907, p. 46. Europeans
benefit, without contributing, in respect of this expenditure on roads.

STATEMENT GIVING PARTICULARS OF PASS LAWS IN FORCE IN THE TRANSVAAL AND ESTIMATED REVENUE THEREFROM

Source.	Law or Regulation.	Substance of Section.	Estimated Annual Receipts.
PASSES:— (a) General passes	Section 8 of Proclamation 18, Admn. 1903.	Any native proceeding for work within his district, or going on his own business beyond the district, must provide himself with a travelling pass, on which a fee of 1s. is charged.	£230,000
	Section 16 of Proclamation 18, Admn. 1903.	Duplicates of travelling passes which have been lost may be obtained on paying a fee of 1s.	
(b) In labour districts	Section 23 of Proclamation 18, Admn. 1903.	Every native engaged by a labour agent and brought to work in a labour district must, within three days of his arrival, be registered and take out a passport. The sum of 1s, is charged for such registration.	
	Section 29 of Proclamation 18, Admn. 1903.	In labour districts a monthly fee of 2s. is payable by the *employer* on each native whom he employs. This fee is payable by the *native* if he is a daily labourer or carries on a trade or calling of his own.	
	Section 34 of Proclamation 18, Admn. 1903.	Duplicates of lost passports are issued on payment of a fee of 1s.	
(c) On public diggings (not proclaimed as labour districts).	Section 150 of Law 15 of 1899 (Gold Law).	Natives within public diggings must take out monthly passes, for which they are charged 1s. This fee will be abolished by the new Gold Law, which does not provide for the issue of such passes.	

in Cape Colony a tax of 2s. per annum is imposed on hut-
tax payers, to be used by the Divisional Council for
road rates.[1]   Boards of Management of native reserves
in the Orange River Colony may levy a location tax not
exceeding £1 in any year on each coloured male person
between the ages of 16 and 60, resident within the reserve.[2]

It will thus be seen that the annual income derived from
the natives (including £1,000,000 for hut- and poll-taxes and
£500,000 for customs duties) may be estimated at about
£2,000,000.   How much of this sum can fairly be treated
as expended directly or indirectly for their benefit?   It is
impossible to answer this question satisfactorily.   Details
are obtainable as to the amounts expended on their education and other matters ; but it is impossible to apportion
to them, with any approach to accuracy, their fair share of
the expenses of the administration of the country.[3]   In
Basutoland, a country which is a purely native reserve, and
where the whole of such expenses are borne by the natives,
there is an annual surplus of income over expenditure.
It may fairly be claimed on behalf of the native that
in Cape Colony, Natal, the Transvaal, the Orange River
Colony, and Rhodesia, he is entitled to have more spent
on him.   In particular, the grants made in aid of his
education, which at present appear wholly insufficient,
should be increased.   A policy in this direction has been
recently initiated in North-Western Rhodesia.   Mr.
R. T. Coryndon, the Administrator, in his report for the

[1] Act No. 30 of 1899, section 25.
[2] O.R.C. Native Reserves Management Ordinance, 1907.
[3] One of the subjects referred to the Natal Native Affairs Commission,
1906-7, was " the cost of administration and the fair share therein of
the native population, with particular reference to the sufficiency or
otherwise of the present contributions to revenue by natives."   The
Commission reported that " as the proportion of the cost of administration fairly chargeable to the natives can only be assumed, no attempt
will be made to answer this part of the question."

year 1906, states that "with the approval of the Secretary of State for the Colonies, a ' Trust Fund ' has been formed of a certain proportion of the native tax received, and this fund is to be expended in works for the direct benefit of the native population. Already the building of a technical school at Lealui has been commenced, native artisans from North-Eastern Rhodesia have been engaged as teachers, and in the coming year a school for the teaching of English will be established at or near Lealui."[1]

In considering the question of the taxation of the native in British South Africa it must be remembered that it is expedient to maintain, so far as possible, methods of taxation to which he has gradually grown accustomed. Like the white man, he readily contributes to the revenue his just share through channels which by long usage he has grown to recognise as part and parcel of the conditions of his life. He views with suspicion the imposition of a new tax or the increase of an existing one.

In this connection it seems well to consider the position in Natal and the effect of the recent poll-tax, which became due for collection on January 1, 1906. There is evidence that for some years the natives of Natal have not found it altogether easy to pay their taxes. Something must be put down to reluctance and to the feelings of dissatisfaction and suspicion which seem to have been growing in the native mind. On the other hand, the magistrates reported in 1904 that in the Vryheid division and in three of the Zululand divisions, hut-tax could not be collected on account of real poverty.[2] From Estcourt it was reported[3] that considering the great scarcity of food when hut-tax was collected, they had paid remarkably well. The levy of the poll-tax increased the irritation, and Mr. R. H. Addison, the magistrate for the Estcourt Division, states in his

[1] British South Africa Company's Report, 1905-6, p. 52.
[2] Natal Blue Book on Native Affairs, 1904, p. ix.   [3] *Ibid.* p. 16.

report for the year 1905 that [1] " the event which created
the greatest stir amongst the natives was the proclamation
of the poll-tax.   To say it was generally received with the
submission with which other promulgations from the Government are received would be telling an untruth.   Its reception may be summarised under the following heads :
(1) A general declaration from all natives residing on
location and private lands of their difficulty in meeting
present taxes and rents to the Government and their landlords respectively. (2) The removal from their sons of their
obligation to the kraal head of providing the hut-tax
by reason of the poll-tax being imposed on them.   No
community in the world likes taxation.   There is no doubt
that the poll-tax is in great disfavour among the natives."

Other circumstances have rendered the burden of taxation more irksome during recent years.   Rents paid by
natives for the occupation of private lands are now very
high.   The squatters' rent on Crown lands in Natal Proper
was increased from £1 to £2 per hut by Act No. 48 of
1903 ; and by regulations under the Mission Reserves Act,
1903, a rent of £3 per annum [2] was imposed in respect of
every hut or dwelling situate in a Mission Reserve.   It may
also be noted that a dog-tax of 5s. per annum was collected
for the first time in Zululand during the year 1905.[3]   Natives
in Natal and Zululand are also called out in large numbers
by the Governor, as supreme chief, to supply labour at low
wages for public works or for the general needs of the
Colony.[4]

This unsatisfactory state of affairs has been carefully
examined by the Natal Native Affairs Commission, 1906-7,
which in its recently issued report states that : [5]

[1] Natal Blue Book on Native Affairs, 1905, p. 11.
[2] This rent has been reduced recently to 30s. per annum.
[3] Natal Blue Book on Native Affairs, 1905, p. iii.
[4] See Chapter I.
[5] Report of Natal Native Affairs Commission, 1906-7, p. 33.

" Poll-tax was objected to, as was to be expected, not only because it was a new burden, but because it was making the sons less inclined to assist their fathers than formerly. Mutuality of interest and reciprocity of assistance was, in kraal-life, a very real and active principle, children being required by enforced custom to account for their earnings to their fathers ; but the force and observance of this commendable custom have for long been on the wane, the young men spending much of their wages upon themselves. They have made this tax, which is personal to themselves, a reason for contributing less to the parental store, according to the statements of old men, repeated time after time and in many places. The generality of the statement consequently lends it credibility. It should be recalled that this tax was imposed by Parliament at the ordinary session of 1905, the year following the taking of the census. The general enumeration connected with the census was resented by the natives, who, not understanding its true import, were naturally suspicious of the intention of the Government. Great pains were taken to allay their fears that it meant neither confiscation nor fresh impositions, but merely a counting. Had there been a body like the proposed Council for Native Affairs to report upon such a measure, and to describe what effect it would have upon the native, particular stress would, undoubtedly, have been laid upon the repeated asseverations of the census officers and the reflections of the natives thereon. Incidents of this nature augment distrust, and emphasise the wisdom of diffusing information regarding the intention of Government, of studying native feeling, and of consulting native opinion.

" The object and proper incidence of the poll-tax upon themselves were, unfortunately, imperfectly, and, perhaps, erroneously conveyed to them. It was baldly represented as a capitation- or head-tax, which, by a simple mental transposition, became converted to a payment for 'the head'; which was as simply followed by the question, 'Why should I pay for my head; is it not my own? and if I have to pay for my head this year, why not for my hands or feet next year?' Whereas, it should have been described to them as a tribute due to the Government by the young unmarried men, the wage-earners, who were not contributing their proportion of taxation.

"The advantages of simplicity of policy, and continuity as well as consistency of action, having been fully demonstrated, it is advisable to adhere to well-established methods, if working well, before resorting to new modes for attaining the same object. As the hut-tax is well understood and regularly collected, with remarkably few evasions, an addition to it would have been better received than the introduction of a novel, and, as it turns out, an imperfectly understood form of taxation. In accordance, therefore, with these views, a consolidation of the several items of taxation is advocated, to take the form of an increased hut-tax, upon a higher scale in locations, and a lower scale in Zululand and upon farms. In view of the substantial gain to the natives which would follow the introduction of the proposed changes in ameliorating their condition and strengthening their control, the merging of taxation should be so arranged as to result in an increase of the total amount of their direct contributions to the Treasury. A large increase thereto is neither proposed nor expected.

"Concurrently with an increased hut-tax, relief should be given in other directions, viz. by abolishing the rent of £2 per hut on Crown lands (now a vanishing amount), the tax upon the bachelor's hut, a modification of the dog-tax, and the corvée or compulsory labour on public works."

Much might be done to alleviate the present position of

the native in Natal and Zululand by the adoption of these
recommendations, provided that the proposed increase in
the hut-tax was not excessive.

In considering these questions of taxation, it is well
to bear in mind the wise counsel of Lord Cromer, who, in
his Soudan report for the year 1904, when advising as
to the course to be pursued, writes : " In deciding what
general policy is to be adopted in countries such as
Egypt and the Soudan, low taxation should be the key-
stone of the political arch.   It brings general tranquillity
in its train.   It is an essential preliminary to steady and
continuous moral and material improvement.   It allows,
either at once or eventually, of the adoption, without
serious danger to the State, of a policy in other matters
which is in general conformity with the liberal views and
traditions of the British Government and of the British
nation.   Expenditure on objects, however desirable in
themselves, should, I venture to think, be rejected, or at
all events postponed, rather than that the principle of
maintaining taxes at a low figure should be in any degree
infringed.   That is the policy which, for more than twenty
years, has been adopted in Egypt, and for some seven
years in the Soudan. . . .

" I am aware that the policy which I have briefly
described above, and of which, during the whole of my
administrative career, I have been a persistent advocate,
is slow in its operation, and that its application appears at
times to produce no immediate results.   The counter-
policy of high State expenditure, which is often urged
upon the governing authorities from many influential
quarters, is often, to all outward appearance, more productive of immediate consequences.   On the other hand,
I venture to maintain that the advantages secured by the
former are far more solid and durable than any which can
be obtained under the latter plan of action."

The imposition of taxes for the purpose of compelling natives to work has in the past been strongly advocated. This method of increasing the supply of labour has now happily been discredited as both impolitic and unjust. But the partial exemption of farm natives in the Transvaal from the poll-tax, shows that taxation is still regarded in that Colony as a means of regulating the labour supply; and in Rhodesia a recent Commission has advised the exemption from taxation of all natives who are in the service of white employers for a specified portion of the year. This system of relieving native employees from liability for taxes needs to be carefully watched. A reduction of taxes in the case of the farm natives may be justified on the ground of the smallness of their earnings. But on this ground many other natives would have a strong claim for similar treatment. To grant exemptions of this kind mainly with a view to the convenience of white employers is a dangerous practice, which might easily be abused. It might, in fact, lead to the establishment of the mischievous labour-tax under a new form.

CHAPTER IV

ADMINISTRATION

BY SIR GODFREY Y. LAGDEN, K.C.M.G.,

Late Commissioner for Native Affairs in the Transvaal, and formerly Resident Commissioner of Basutoland.

§ 1. INTRODUCTORY

IN dealing with the question of Administration of Native Affairs in British South Africa it is necessary, while considering and comparing the different systems and enactments, to trace first of all the territorial distribution of the natives, and to refer to a few general features in respect of their absorption under civilised rule.

The native population to which this chapter relates is distributed as follows:

	Population.	Density per Square Mile in Reserves.
Cape Colony	1,424,787	50·36
Natal (including Zululand) . .	904,041	33·35 [4]
Transvaal (including Swaziland) .	1,030,029 [1]	24·00 [5]
Orange River Colony . . .	235,466	132·81
Southern Rhodesia . . .	591,197 [2]	6·80
Basutoland	347,731 [3]	33·78
Bechuanaland Protectorate . .	119,411	·78
Total	4,652,662	

[1] Includes 133,745 labourers temporarily resident.
[2] Includes 20,367 labourers temporarily resident.
[3] Excludes 20,000 absent at labour on census-taking.
[4] Density on reserves in Natal 66·48; in Zululand 19·58.
[5] Density on reserves in Transvaal 59·4; in Swaziland 12·9.

These figures (which do not include "coloured" or half-caste people) are taken from the latest standing records in collective form, viz. from the Report of the South African Native Affairs Commission published in 1905.

The colonies and possessions above named came under some kind of effective occupation or administration approximately in the following years :

Cape Colony, 1814.   Natal, 1843.
Orange River Colony, 1848.   Transvaal, 1852.
Basutoland, 1868.   Bechuanaland Protectorate, 1885.
Rhodesia, 1888.

It is material to note these dates, because they serve to indicate the period during which the aboriginals have been more or less under civilised control. Throughout that period the administrations have been composed, sometimes of British, sometimes of Dutch, whose ideas of the management of natives were not always identical.

It was only natural that, following upon a series of ruptures between the two European races which ensued before and after slavery was abolished by the passing of the Emancipation Act in 1834, a strong sentiment should have animated the Dutch when they came to frame their own native laws and regulations to be carried out in their own independent Republics.

The pioneer settlers were few, scattered, and unprotected, and it is quite intelligible that they deemed it necessary to make their early laws affecting aboriginals rigorous and restrictive. Their doctrine was demonstrated in the Fundamental Law, in which a prominent article declared : " The people will admit of no equality of persons of colour with the white inhabitants in State or Church." That ring of stern domination may be traced throughout all the early Republican legislation.

But other considerations at times operated to prompt variation in the form of legislation. In some parts the state and capacity of the natives were determining factors. Again, instances were not lacking where rigour of rule was increased or relaxed according as the Kafirs had offered obstinate resistance, and were only subdued after they had perpetrated cruelties and inflicted great hardships on the settlers, or had surrendered readily ; or, indeed, had ceded territory with the mutual understanding for incorporation of their land upon terms carrying with it certain independent rights. Yet another element influenced law-makers, viz. : the fact whether or not newly annexed tribes were indissolubly bound up with the tribal system. Finally, much turned upon the Constitution, for, whereas in that of the Cape Colony natives were accorded equal franchise rights with white people, subject to property and other qualifications, in the late Republics they were debarred from direct representation.

Under such circumstances, different laws, usages, and systems were adopted to suit the varying sensibilities and conditions which the primitive Governments had to take into account.

With one consent, however, all Governments recognised the principle that class legislation for natives was essential, both in their own interests and in that of the Europeans, relating to such matters as tenure of land, direct taxation, passes, liquor, etc., which, with little exception, resulted in laws that came into common use, though the form of them was not identical.

Another point in common was that the Head of the State, whether the Governor of a British colony or the President of a Republic, has nearly always been clothed with authority as Supreme Chief of the native population. Similarly, there was co-ordination in respect of the employment of officers variously termed Resident Magistrates, Landrosts, or Commissioners, as the mediums through whom Government control over the natives was exercised.

These officers were allowed a wide latitude, and were held
responsible either to the Supreme Chief direct, or to the
Governor in Council through one of the highest officers of
State holding ministerial rank.

§ 2. EXISTING LAWS AND ADMINISTRATIVE SYSTEMS

To discuss in detail the many laws and regulations of
force in the South African Dependencies for the management and control of the natives would require much more
space than the limits of this chapter permit. It pretends
only to summarise the legal and administrative systems.

All of the colonies and possessions of South Africa are,
or have been at one time or another, under Crown Colony
government, with the exception of Rhodesia, where, as
regards native affairs, considerable powers are, under the
Royal Charter, reserved to the High Commissioner for
South Africa.

The whole of the *Cape Colony*, including what is known
as the Transkeian or Native Territories, is under Responsible Government, the portfolio of Native Affairs being
held by the Prime Minister, who is answerable to Parliament
for them.

The necessity has always been strongly recognised by
that Colony for elasticity of native administration in those
parts where the population is dense and the special
conditions seemed to warrant it. For that purpose, legislation for the Transkeian Territories has continuously been
exercised by Governor's Proclamations, unless Parliament
deems it urgent to extend by express provision the application of any Act beyond the Kei.

In that sphere, also, greater latitude is allowed to
magistrates in tolerating native customs, and adjudicating
under certain circumstances upon dowry questions which

cannot be entertained in the law courts of the Colony proper where native law and custom are ignored. There is, however, no written code of native law.

For the better treatment of those criminal offences peculiar to local native conditions a Penal Code was specially enacted in 1886. It follows the lines of the Statute and Common Law of the Colony, and aims at finality. It makes specific provision for the constitution and summoning of combined courts of magistrates with extended powers, and for the employment of native assessors, with a view to the advantages derivable from their observations and particularly in the examination of witnesses. This Criminal Code has been found of the highest value not only in the Cape Colony but in adjacent native territories where the spirit of it has been embraced.

We have thus a dividing line in the form of administration, the occasion for which has appealed to the Government and people of the Cape Colony. No such administrative boundary exists so clearly in any other colony, for the reason that segregation elsewhere is not so distinctly marked. But it plainly indicates the importance attached by the premier Colony to the necessity of affording the natives rapid access to Courts of Justice, inexpensive means of litigation, and a sympathetic method of government.

In the Transkei, as in the Colony proper, the head of the District is the Resident Magistrate, whose office corresponds as regards purely native work to that of Native Commissioners or Assistant Commissioners in certain other territories to be hereafter referred to. But these Resident Magistrates are called upon to perform a variety of work connected with Europeans as well. They are alone and entirely responsible to Government for the administration of justice, collection of taxes, settlement of land and licence questions, and the maintenance of order. They have a few minor officials and police for district use.

The system has admittedly worked smoothly and efficiently. But in regard to the designation "Resident Magistrates" it must be observed for comparative purposes that the bulk of the work is native, a limited number only of white people being resident for trade, industry, and other local business pursuits.

In the *Colony of Natal*, which gained Responsible Government in 1893, we find an entirely different order of things. The Secretary for Native Affairs is a Cabinet Minister.

In 1891 a Code of Native Law was enacted which, subject to exemption under certain conditions, applies to the whole native population (Zululand excepted, where the Code is recognised without being legally operative).

By an Article of the Code no native falling under the operation of Native Law can reside in the Colony unless he becomes a member of a tribe; and a tribe is defined as a community of not less than twenty kraals under leadership of a chief, who is recognised as such by the Supreme Chief.

At first sight it appears to simplify the means and methods of government if the natives as a whole are brought under one codified law. The system has its advantages and disadvantages, its advocates and its opponents.

The administration of this Code and the government of the Natal natives are facilitated by the fact that the Governor of the Colony is *ex-officio* Supreme Chief of the native population. As such he is endowed with the power to punish by fine or imprisonment, and to remove or depose chiefs; he is not in that capacity subject to the Supreme Court, or any other Court of Law in the Colony, for or by reason of any order, proclamation, act or matter committed, ordered, permitted, or done by him.

Without the vesting of absolute power in some

exalted individual it would be practically impossible
to carry out satisfactorily and enforce a Code of this
character. Generally speaking, the power implied is
that which a paramount chief formerly enjoyed under
the naked tribal system before it became absorbed under
civilised government, excepting, of course, the power to kill
or maltreat.

The Code itself is comprehensive in construction, and,
after the definition of terms and of the powers of the
Supreme Chief and those in authority under him, deals
in an exhaustive form with : the duties, powers, and privileges of chiefs and headmen in their relation to the people ;
the kraal system ; status ; inheritance and succession ;
marriages, divorce and lobolo ; land tenure ; courts, civil
and criminal ; procedure ; offences, and a variety of other
matters which are essential to its fulfilment.

It is in itself a most commendable instrument, and will
always stand out as a record of admirable intention on· the
part of the Natal Government and Colonists to preserve
to the native people what was good in their own primitive
system, and what, for a stage in their history, was firmly
believed to be the soundest policy in reconciling barbarians
steeped in wild tradition to civilised conventionalities.

At one time officers styled Administrators of Native
Law were selected for their technical knowledge, and
deputed to deal with cases arising under the Code ; but
these have latterly been discontinued, the resident magistrates now assuming entire responsibility for it.   Whilst so
doing, they are vested, as in the Cape, with District control
affecting both Europeans and natives.   With the exception
of the urban areas, however, the great bulk of their work
pertains to natives.

In the *Orange River Colony* the native population is
fragmentary, being for the most part dispersed amongst
European farmers or settled in towns.

Their affairs are administered under the common law of
the country. There is a Native Adviser of the Government
stationed at the capital, with a small assisting staff, and
two small Reserves superintended by special officers.
Native law finds no place, except that it is tolerated in so
far as the natives may arrange to agree to it amongst
themselves, and effect settlements by friendly arbitration.
The resident magistrates adjudicate upon all district
matters.

In the *Transvaal* the business of the Native Affairs
Department now forms a principal function of one of
the Cabinet Ministers under the new Constitution. The
administrative system assumes a shape which differs
somewhat from that of previously named colonies, yet
retains some of the essentials of each. In effect it has
a standard law which, while not prescribing or validating
a definite code, provides, amongst other things, for the
recognition of existing native law and custom not inconsistent with the general principles of civilisation, or not in
conflict with the accepted principles of justice. This law
endows the Governor with power to exercise over chiefs
and natives all power and authority which, in accordance
with native custom, are given to any paramount chief.

It will be observed, therefore, that the Governor of the
Transvaal has apparently a position closely corresponding
to that of the Governor of Natal, without the aid or
encumbrance, as the case may be, of a code. Yet he lacks
what the Natal legislators evidently considered to be the
backbone of their Code, viz. that the Governor should be
protected by the indemnity clause, to which allusion has
been made. In the absence of such a clause, the Transvaal native administration suffers from the risk of vexatious
appeals, and is hampered in consequence.

What native law and custom in the Transvaal consists
of is, then, unwritten, and the interpretation of it is left

to the knowledge and discretion of those enjoined to administer it. This is a flexible order of things which adapts itself to the circumstances of the country. Though the standard law is faulty in some respects, it is by no means without merit.

Both under the Republican and present Governments in the Transvaal the policy has been to employ as administrators of native affairs, in those districts where the natives are massed in any considerable number, native Commissioners and sub-Commissioners, whose sole and undivided attention is devoted to that class of work, the Resident Magistrates acting as such *ex-officio*, as landrosts did formerly, where the presence of expert officers can be dispensed with.

In *Basutoland* and *Bechuanaland Protectorate* the basis of administration is practically identical. These territories are governed by Resident Commissioners, under direction of the High Commissioner for South Africa, the latter possessing the legislative authority which is exercised by proclamation.

The chiefs adjudicate in cases between native and native, with a right of appeal to the Courts of Assistant Commissioners, and of final appeal to the Resident Commissioner.

To these Courts all cases between Europeans and natives are brought, unless, by mutual consent of parties, the Chief's Court is agreed upon, in which event there is a proviso that no European who shall have consented to submit himself to jurisdiction of a native chief shall have any right of appeal therefrom.

The Resident Commissioner is supported by assistant Commissioners, whom he may summon at discretion to form Combined Courts for the trial of civil or criminal cases. Power is also given to call in native assessors for technical purposes relating to native law and custom, and

for assistance in hearing cases, but the finding of the Court
is vested exclusively in the presiding officer.

In each of these territories the laws of the Cape Colony,
up to a certain date, are proclaimed to be in force as
nearly as the circumstances of the country will permit.

Southern Rhodesia, embracing the provinces of Matabeleland and Mashonaland, is governed under an Order in
Council, which provides for a Constitution with large
powers of control to the High Commissioner for South
Africa. By a Proclamation of 1891, the laws of the Cape
Colony in operation prior to that date were adopted, and
are of effect as far as the circumstances of the country
permit.

The Native Department is administered by the Secretary
for Native Affairs, the duties of that office hitherto having
been performed by the Administrator-in-Chief of the
Territory.

The two provinces are each under control of a chief
Native Commissioner, appointed under approval of the
High Commissioner, and assistant Commissioners, all of
whom give their undivided attention to native affairs.

There is no established code of native law, but due
regard is had to those laws and customs to which the
natives are habituated.

Apart from the European officers in the various
colonies and possessions referred to, a force of native police
has everywhere proved of immense benefit to the Administrations. They are recruited from the local clans,
with whom they are allied in blood and sympathy, and
act as mediums of communication between the masses
and the Government. By their capacity for gaining
intelligence, and by loyal behaviour, they have, both
in times of trouble and of peace, been factors of the
highest order in the successful control of our subject
races.

§ 3. JURISDICTION AND DUTIES OF EUROPEAN OFFICERS AND NATIVE CHIEFS

Large powers are conferred upon the Resident Commissioners of Basutoland and Bechuanaland Protectorate. They are entitled to exercise jurisdiction in, and adjudicate upon, all causes, suits, and actions whatever, civil or criminal. They are empowered to review and correct the proceedings of all Courts or officers in their territories in all cases. No Supreme Courts are vested with higher powers, and nowhere perhaps is finality so cheaply and rapidly achieved.

Their assistant Commissioners have also a wide jurisdiction, which is defined, not by law, but by the terms of their commissions. It is thus possible to give to experienced officers larger powers and latitude than are given to juniors undergoing training.

Resident Magistrates throughout South Africa have limited jurisdiction not exceeding, as a rule, the power to imprison for six months, sentences in excess of three months being subject to review by Judges of the Supreme Court. Extended jurisdiction is given in some colonies under Cattle Theft Repression Acts.

Native Commissioners in Rhodesia exercise the powers conferred upon Magistrates. It is specifically laid down in respect of Rhodesia that native Commissioners shall control the natives through their tribal chiefs and headmen.

Though a common practice to do this in other territories, it is not so commanded in this clear and distinct form.

In the Transvaal native Commissioners have much smaller powers of jurisdiction than are given to Resident Magistrates or to the Assistant Commissioners in native territories.

The powers conferred upon and exercised by native chiefs and headmen vary considerably.

In Basutoland and Bechuanaland it is competent for any native chief to be appointed to adjudicate upon and try cases, civil and criminal, in which natives are concerned, and to exercise jurisdiction in such manner and within such limits as may be defined by rules and regulations established by the Resident Commissioner, who is empowered to make such rules. Chiefs are so appointed and so act.

In Natal chiefs have power under the Code to try all civil cases (divorces excepted) between natives, and are entitled to claim and exercise the privileges appertaining to Courts of Law in respect of disobedience of their orders or contempt of their persons or Courts, and may for such offences impose fines. They may further inflict fines for neglect of orders which they as deputies of the Supreme Chief enunciate to their people.

In the Transvaal, chiefs appointed by Government are authorised to decide civil disputes between natives under native law, and also civil matters referred to them by white people against natives.

In all native territories obligations are, for administrative purposes, imposed upon chiefs more or less of the following description : maintenance of order and good conduct of tribe ; supply of men for defence in suppression of disorder ; notification of crimes and offences, suspicious deaths and epidemics ; the cognition and control of suspicious strangers and strange cattle ; the publication of laws and orders.

Upon due fulfilment of such obligations certain privileges accrue, principal of which are : rank, salaries, court fees and the right to respect and obedience of their people, which, though not made compulsory by law, is almost invariably accorded when the conduct of the chief deserves it.

Headmen in a lesser degree partake of the powers, obligations, and privileges of chiefs according to their family influence, capacity, and following. They are not

strictly empowered to determine cases which are, nevertheless, in minor matters frequently taken to them for
arbitrament with knowledge and consent of chiefs.

But in Natal, under the Code, kraal heads, whose
is distinct from headmen, have important duties as
guardians of minors; as constables within kraal precincts,
having power to arrest, suspected persons committing
offences against person or property, or rioting, or intro-
ducing intoxicating liquors; and in execution of their
duties they may inflict corporal punishment for purpose
of correction, and to maintain peace and good order in their
kraals, and for any other just cause; however, they
are given a power which is denied had long been
magistrates in South Africa.

§ 4. COUNCILS AS AN AID TO ADMINISTRATION

In the foregoing pages an outline has been sketched of
the general and varied forms of native administration and
the personnel employed to carry it out.

It will now be pertinent to consider briefly in what
degree the natives share in it by means of Councils or
consultation.

We have seen that in certain territories they are allowed
to determine cases in Courts of their own, to be called in
as assessors in higher Courts, and to be utilised as political
police.

In 1894 a great advance was made by the Cape Colony,
always the pioneer in matters concerning native progress,
by passing, at the instance of the late Mr. Rhodes, the Glen
Grey Act.

That Act was made to operate in certain Districts of
the Transkei which lent themselves to the prospect of a
successful experiment.

The District of Glen Grey comprises the tract of country

lying between the Divisions of Queenstown, Wodehouse,
and Indwe, and contained a considerable native population,
had established itself in locations and become
med to individual la   tenure under the system
ated by Governor S   eorge Grey, who allocated
er the Kafir war

: may be sumr   to involve in principle :

dividual tit¹

ecc 'tion   la of primogeniture ;

o   government by means of

xcs and vote expenditure.

manifest that, although in Kaffraria the
natives clung tenaciously to their traditional
s and superstitions, and were partial to the use of red
clay as a cosmetic, a numerous section of them were fast
rising above it, and were winning, by their intellectual
capacity, character, and persistency, the esteem and confidence of the Magistrates and Government. It was to
them that the Act was designed chiefly to apply, with the
idea that they in turn would lead the red heathen in the
direction of higher ideals.

By lodging with a body of intelligent natives the power
and responsibility to conduct a portion at any rate of
their own affairs, under the guidance of European officers,
a large burden was shifted from the shoulders of Government, and it lay with those so endowed to suggest changes
for betterment and for development on their own lines of
thought.

With this general idea, the Act provides for :

(a) A General Council, consisting of members elected by
each District, the Government nominating a proportion,
with the District Resident Magistrates as *ex-officio* members ;
the whole presided over by the Chief Magistrate of the
Transkei.

(*b*) District Councils, composed of men nominated partly by the District Headmen and partly by Government, with the Resident Magistrate as Chairman.

To these Councils are committed many of the duties which in other parts devolve entirely upon the Administration. It contemplates to give the native people a direct interest in their own affairs, to educate them to the performance of public work, and to teach them to bea and remedy if they can, grievances which were formerly showered upon their rulers.

It is claimed with justification that these Councils have proved a success in the Transkei in lightening the burder of Government and broadening the native mind. Tha they have served a good purpose in easing the adminis trative machine all evidence goes to show.

In 1903 a Select Committee of the Cape House of Assembly appointed to inquire into the working and administration of the Glen Grey Act reported, *inter alia*, as follows :

" Speaking generally, ... your Committee are convinced that the operations of the Act have been, as they were intended to be, most beneficial to the natives concerned. Individual tenure and local self-government have done much, and will in the future do more, to lead the aboriginal natives in the path of improvement."

But, while admitting the beneficial effect of this Act, in so far as it has been applied in a limited way in the Cape Colony, it is not to be assumed that its application could (in a summary way) be made general in South Africa, where the circumstances are so varied and the environment not always favourable. The Transkei lends itself to the idea in a way that cannot easily be followed.

Basutoland, however, has reached a stage when the Constitution, the people, and the country combine to favour the adoption of the Council system.

There are obstacles, in that it has a paramount chief and powerful chieftains, all of whom are bound to be opposed in spirit to any scheme calculated to dispossess or lessen the power they enjoy.

Former paramount chiefs foresaw the internal dangers that might arise as the native mind grew and became restless under the restraints of vassalage, and advocated in their declining years the establishment of a Council with influence sufficient to control unruly passions.

Yet in their own lifetimes they hesitated to press for it in such a way as might lead to the curbing of their own powers.

Nevertheless, a Council has, after the proposal was digested for twenty years, been recently formed. It consists of about 100 representatives, selected partly by the nation and partly by Government.

Its principal functions are to ventilate opinions and grievances and confer with the Administration. One of its early acts was to frame a code for the guidance of chiefs in respect of, amongst other things : the rights of individuals ; the use and obligations of land ; Court procedure, succession, and inheritance.

This Council has, happily, avoided attempts at drastic change, and, catching the temper of the people, has tended in a useful way to cultivate their imagination and promote good order.

It may have a great future as the people progress on temperate lines, and, while bringing to the Administration the support of public opinion and suggestion, serves as an object-lesson to South Africa.

§ 5. THE FUTURE

It remains now before closing this chapter to record a few thoughts which suggest themselves upon a subject which affords so much food for reflection.

No doubt exists in the minds of those acquainted with the comparative conditions and affairs of the natives of South Africa to-day that they are going through the trying ordeal of change. How they will emerge from it remains to be seen.

Under the influences of Christian teaching, education, and contact with civilisation, the minds of all are opening, and the intelligence of a good many is ripening. They are yearning for sympathy, and are leaning hopefully upon their European rulers for assistance and guidance in their development.

It is a moment when the efforts and aspirations of those who are struggling to improve may with advantage to all concerned be directed upon lines suitable to their environment.

Sectional opposition may always be expected, and will be offered to any action designed to enlarge their status beyond that of hewers of wood and drawers of water. But signs are not wanting from all quarters of the subcontinent that their rulers and the leaders of civilised thought are ready, indeed anxious, to examine native problems most carefully, and to extend to them fair and generous consideration.

But no amount of fair consideration can alter the fact that, although the native races are closely allied in character and language, they are suffering at our hands from a bewildering variety of forms of administration.

The question of South African Federation is visibly being forced into the region of practical politics. It forms a principal topic upon many public platforms. Before Federation becomes a reality, the assimilation in some preliminary degree of laws and systems for the management of natives must engage the profound attention of the Colonial Governments and people.

That it will be a delicate task to harmonise throughout

South Africa the direction of Native Affairs and establish uniformity of practice is unquestionable.

Prominent amongst the difficulties to confront those who first deliberate is the factor of chieftainship which still retains a powerful hold upon the natives and continues to be intermittently employed as a means of government.

As time goes on the aboriginals will, as a result of education and enlightenment, more and more manifest their dislike to the old barbarous habits and customs, and fret under the yoke of their chiefs, who will gradually disappear from the stage as actors and be no more seen.

The chiefs will, however, during the feudal history of the tribes have performed great services, entitling them to the respect and devotion which the great bulk of their followers have always cherished towards them.

There are many who believe that no real progress can be made unless and until the chiefs are summarily deposed. But, if an apology for the past is necessary, the whole lesson of history is to teach us that the early condition of all nations has been characterised by personal and autocratic leadership, and that evolution, to be sound, must proceed by stages admitting of healthy and calm growth ; it may be retarded, and its course deflected by unsuitable treatment and haste.

Abundant signs have been given that the authority of chiefs is resented by sections in every colony who are either led by native agitators to resist it, or are persuaded by law agents to defy it by appeal to the superior Courts where political expediency is not held in favour, and where there is always an inclination to strike at systems inimical to European law and practice.

The young men, too, chafe under customs which render them liable to be sent out to labour at the instance of chiefs, who derive pay from recruiting agencies for each man supplied, and who compel them to perform retainers' duty in cultivating the lands.

All this tends to shake the influence of chiefs and break it down.

But it is wiser to let the leaven of free thought do its own work than to endanger the peace by violent changes that might give to chieftainship a common cause to unite in resisting them. Hitherto the common cause has been discreetly avoided.

In disturbing the influence of chiefs over their people it must be borne in mind that with it goes the whole chain of responsibility which has proved so invaluable in the past in maintaining order, suppressing crime, and preserving useful control over wild people capable of becoming easily excited to acts of rebellion.

It may be taken as fairly assured that any general adoption of the Natal Code system is regarded as undesirable and unlikely, as being retrogressive in character and subversive of progress. Moreover, the powers given to chiefs and headmen under that code cannot be reconciled with modern law and practice.

Its opponents urge with some force that, in trying to save trouble and simplify administration by codifying native law, the true development of the aboriginals has been hindered and sacrificed. The controversy is one of the highest moment, affecting as it does so vitally the whole order of evolution.

It is of paramount importance so long as the rude laws and customs of the natives are suffered that they should continue to have not only minor courts of their own, but special courts and qualified officers devoted to the management of their affairs. These officers require power, assimilated if possible in all territories, to hear and determine native cases with promptness and finality and at little cost to the parties.

If one point was brought out more significantly than another during the evidence before the late South African Native Affairs Commission it was that, under existing con-

ditions and systems, it is essential, in the interests of peace
and contentment, to provide for the interpretation on
appeal of native laws by officers in authority who enjoy
the confidence of the natives.   A remarkable illustration of
the urgent necessity of this was furnished in the Cape
Colony, where in one large District a magistrate had
for over twenty years, with the knowledge and consent of
Government, done magnificent work in settling native
cases by pure arbitration, all parties agreeing to be bound
by his decision in the absence of a Court lawfully established to deal with such matters.

The preamble to the Transvaal Standard Law enacted by
the Republic in 1885 may here be quoted as embodying
the useful principle which has largely guided South Africa
in the past.   It recites as follows :

" Whereas it is necessary to provide for the better treatment and management of the natives by placing them
under special supervision, and for the proper administration
of justice amongst them until they shall be able to understand and appreciate such duties and responsibilities as
they may reasonably be deemed capable of undertaking in
obedience to the general law. . . ."

It may be that we are close to the parting of the ways ;
that the toleration of native law and custom is nearing its
end and that chieftainship, as a recognised channel for the
conduct of native affairs, will be replaced by magistrates
and native commissioners.

These officers would in such case have to take up a
heavy burden, and upon their character and methods much
would depend.   No doubt they would as far as possible
follow the best traditions of the old order as regards
paternal care.   But they would require to be strengthened
by an approved policy which empowered them to establish
district councils for consultation and afforded them a distinct
aim in the process of reconciling the natives to the change,

The change will be expensive, as the chiefs now do so much police and other work without pay or support ; but it will have the effect of bringing the native population directly under the Common Law of the country as applied to Europeans.

We may be presumed to be drifting fast in that direction as a solution of the problem to be faced by those who discuss Federation when they endeavour to determine how to arrive at uniformity of administration.

Meanwhile there is need of the utmost caution not to provoke unrest and discontent by rooting up prevailing systems until the native mind is prepared and effective substitutes are in readiness.

When the curtain falls upon native law and custom the natives must, in the absence of direct representation, be heard through Councils similar in character to those now established in the Transkei and Basutoland. They will tend to facilitate administration by bringing into close and sympathetic touch the dominant races who are responsible and the weaker races who are concerned in their own progress and betterment.

NOTE.—Since the above was written and sent to the printer a report, the latest of its kind, has been issued of the Natal Native Affairs Commission, to which a long and comprehensive list of subjects affecting Native Affairs in Natal was referred for inquiry.

Further, in the *Gazette* of January 21, 1908, is published a thoughtful memorandum upon the report by Mr. S. O. Samuelson, Secretary for Native Affairs in Natal.

While it is not the purpose of this chapter to review such papers, a few remarks upon such recent documents, upon which legislation is now being based, may be offered.

The Report endorses certain of the convictions which find brief expression in the preceding pages of this chapter and, amongst other things, it says :

(1) Speaking of the tribal system : " With a full confession of all its defects, political, moral, and social, and as a bar to individual progress, to attempt to sweep it away would be suicidal, and lead to worse evils than now surround it."

(2) The direct control of the natives in general should be entrusted to carefully selected officers imbued with an intense desire for the welfare of the people.

(3) Elasticity of native management is essential ; the course of natural evolution should not be diverted.

(4) The natives are being over-administered and are ignorant of many of the laws which affect themselves.

(5) Native administrators should be more paternal than official : the seat and centre of authority should be visible, permanent, and accessible.

(6) The magistrates are trammelled by law and rule.

(7) The powers and duties of the Supreme Chief should be clearly defined, in the exercise of which he should be free from review or interference.

(8) It should be an objective to establish Village Settlements under an inceptive form of self-government, and to issue conditional land titles, in selected areas (somewhat on the Glen Grey system).

Upon the subject of the retention of the Code of Native Law, the Commission advances no pronounced opinion of its own, beyond saying that a study of it by experts will, in the light of experience and changed circumstances, doubtless lead to several alterations, and that there is need for amendment. It quotes, however, " an almost unanimous expression of opinion by magistrates and others that there *should* be a Code, and that, to secure uniformity, it should have the force of law, and be extended to Zululand."

Mr. Samuelson dissents warmly, for reasons given, from some of the recommendations of the Commission, deeming them to be contradictory in themselves and calculated to make confusion worse.

He takes particular exception to that part which suggests the appointment of native Commissioners, "who should be used to supplant the chiefs. . . . and thus gradually help with other agencies to break down the tribal system"—a system which is previously regarded by the Commission as "a necessary institution, indispensable for the government of the natives." But, while feelingly directing attention to this apparent inconsistency, he adds that, in his opinion, the Report will do more harm than good as calculated to embitter both sections of the community.

I do not share this gloomy view, believing that there is much good to be derived from Commissions like this, which not only place prominently before the public the position of local affairs, but help to form and educate public opinion and to cultivate sympathetic consideration for the natives.

It is not to be expected that the views of any Commission will command entire concurrence and support, seeing how much opinion is divided on what is admittedly a complex question.

As an illustration of administrative anomaly at a time when unification of policy is desired on all sides, we have the Natal Commission recommending the appointment of Native Commissioners separate from the Magistracy, whilst at the same moment a similar grade of officers has, principally from motives of economy, been abolished in the Transvaal after having done sound political work amongst the natives of that Colony.

It is only by anomalies of this character being brought to light that a view of the situation can be properly seen. If it leads to temperate discussion, so much the better.

Native Commissioners are essential as part of the system in some colonies and protectorates. It serves no useful purpose to condemn them as a whole because they do not appear well-placed in other parts.

CHAPTER V

LEGAL STATUS OF NATIVES

§ 1. INTRODUCTORY

THIS chapter describes briefly the legal position or status of the natives as distinguished from that of the whites. The subject, which has many branches, can be discussed here only imperfectly. Theoretically, three very distinct ways of treating the aboriginal natives of a country occupied and governed by a white population may be conceived. They may be treated as if they had no rights, a course rarely, if ever—certainly never avowedly—taken in modern times. They may be treated as a people apart, with laws of their own, to which only they are subject ; the method adopted by most civilised conquerors in recent times towards subject races—a course which presents many advantages, and which can consistently be followed when the aboriginal inhabitants live apart and retain their native laws and customs unimpaired, but one which becomes more and more difficult as their original social organisation breaks up or the force of their own laws is weakened. Or the aboriginal population may be treated exactly as the European population—a policy generally repugnant to people of European descent associated with a black race.[1]

In no country probably have any of these courses been strictly adhered to. Generally there have been com-

---

[1] See paper by Dr. Hermann Hesse as to the course pursued by the German Government in their West African colonies. " Zeitschrift für Kolonialpolitik, Kolonialrecht," etc., 1904, p. 190.

promises and mixtures of all of these policies. Such has been, at all events, the case in South Africa. All the colonies have not acted alike. The same colony has not always followed the same principle at different times. In fact, no consistent course has been followed. In South African legislation there are examples of the second and third courses above described, and there have been many compromises of various kinds.

§ 2. Definitions of Natives

Though the South African colonies have followed no very consistent course, it will appear that there is an approximation towards certain types of legislation. One of the first fruits of the federation may be to bring about similarity of policy in regard to a matter as to which there has been notable diversity.

Who are to be regarded as natives? This question does not admit of a sure and simple answer. The mixture of races has given rise to one set of difficulties. The fact that certain persons have wholly or gradually withdrawn from tribal life gives rise to another class of difficulties. Each colony has looked at the question from its own point of view. The consequence is that the statutory definitions of natives are not at all in agreement.

In Cape Colony there does not seem to be a general definition of " native," but for the purposes of special Acts there are definitions. Thus the definition in Act No. 40, 1902, as to native locations, is: " Any Kafir, Fingo, Zulu, Mosuto, Damara, Hottentot, Bushman, Bechuana, Koranna, or any other aboriginal native of South or Central Africa, but shall not include any native while serving in any of His Majesty's ships and while in uniform." For the purposes of the Liquor Amendment Act (Act No. 28, 1898, sect. 5), "native" is defined as meaning any Kafir, Fingo, Basuto, Damara, Hottentot, Bushman, or Koranna.

In Natal also the definitions vary. As the Natal Native Affairs Commission remarks (p. 19): "A definition has been attempted, in one way or another, by some seven or eight statutes, with a resultant conflict of opinions and confusion of ideas as to what persons or classes fall within the definitions given." The Firearms and Ammunition Act of Natal (Act No. 1, 1906) says: "'Native' means and includes all members of the aboriginal races or tribes of Africa, whether exempted or not from the operation of Native law, and Griquas and Hottentots, and any person whose parents or either of them come under the description of Natives, Griquas, or Hottentots, and the descendants of any such person." According to the Code of Native Law for Natal (Art. 12), "the word 'Native' shall be deemed to mean and to include any member of the aboriginal races or tribes of Africa south of the Equator."

In the Transvaal, by Proclamation No. 37, 1901 (Passes Law), as amended by Ordinance No. 27 of 1903, *native* shall mean "a male person over fourteen years of age both of whose parents are members of some aboriginal race or tribe of Africa"; under Law No. 24 of 1895, "Any person of any kind belonging to or being a descendant of any of the Native races in South Africa." The Liquor Law of the Transvaal (No. 32, 1902) applies to "coloured persons," a vague and wide phrase, which includes Indians (Bosch *v.* Rex, 1904, T.S. p. 57). Under the Transvaal Immorality Act (Ord. 46, 1903, s. 19 (5)) *native* means a person manifestly belonging to any of the native or coloured races of Africa, Asia, America, or St. Helena.

In the Orange River Colony, by Law No. 8 of 1893, s. 8: "coloured person or coloured persons" include "a man or men as well as a woman or women above the age or estimated age of sixteen years of any native tribe in South Africa, and also all coloured persons and all who, in accordance with law or custom, are called coloured persons, or are treated as such, of whatever race or nationality they may be "—obviously a very vague definition.

In Rhodesia, by Regulation No. 240, 1898 (sect. 3), *native* means " any person being, or being a descendant of, an aboriginal native of Africa."

In some legislation (*e.g.* Natal Intoxicating Liquor Act, 1896, Art. 4) there are added the words, " Including liberated Africans, commonly called ' Amandawo.' "

Outside the terms of these statutes and the like, there is an ill-defined power of treating persons with certain racial characteristics as "natives." We quote from a well-known text-writer : " Apart from the statutory definitions of a native it has been laid down—and the decision is fully applicable throughout South Africa—that a person whose general appearance presents the leading characteristics of an aboriginal native might be taken for such, even though it may be shown that there are traces of European blood in such a person." (Reg. *v.* Willet, 12 C.T.R. 238 ; " Nathan's Digest," p. 2519, n.). In Reg. *v.* Willet the question was whether one Rose Coetzee was an aboriginal native within the meaning of "native" in Notice No. 241 of 1901 as to selling intoxicating liquor to an aboriginal native. Coetzee gave evidence that her mother was a " bastard Hottentot " and her father a Boer, and that they were married. There was medical evidence that she " appears to have some European blood." The conviction by the magistrate was upheld, De Villiers, C.J., remarking : " The Court has decided that an admixture of European blood does not prevent a person from being regarded as an aboriginal native if the features of the aboriginal predominate." With such vague tests as the above to apply, some members of the same family might be regarded as natives, some not.

Obviously there has been extreme difficulty in finding a definition applicable to persons very unlike, of different degrees of culture and intelligence and civilisation—a definition which will take account of racial intermixtures as well as degrees of culture. The lines of colour and those of culture do not necessarily, or in fact, coincide. The existence of these differences and the consequent uncertainty as to the legal position of many persons have brought evil with them. A large number of persons, and some of those most inclined to adopt civilised life, are left in an ambiguous condition. The continuance of these differences must strengthen the impression among the natives that they are dealt with in an arbitrary way. In the same category, and subject to the same disabilities, are placed persons with nothing in common but their colour; sometimes persons without even that common trait.

§ 3. EXEMPTED PERSONS

It was long recognised that many natives could not with propriety be treated in the same manner as the ordinary raw Kafir. Of natives falling within the above definitions, many are exempted from the operation of native law. The manner in which, and the conditions upon which, such exemption is obtained vary in the colonies. The grounds of exemption differ much. For the most part they are based on educational qualifications. In Cape Colony every duly registered voter of whatever nationality, tribe, or colour, is so exempt. So are persons with certain educational qualifications. In the other colonies application for such exemptions must be made.

There are many complaints as to the position of the exempted native. He believes that he is unfairly treated ; that while asking for bread he has been given a stone. One disqualification is particularly resented. The Natal legislation of 1865 formed a special class of "exempted natives"—*i.e.* natives who were not subject to native law. The Courts of that Colony have decided that the children of those exempted under the Act of 1865 (Law 28) are not in the same position as their parents—a remarkable anomaly (Mahludi *v.* Rex, 26 N.L.R. p. 298); one strange result being that in the same family there may be children born prior to the grant of the letters who are exempt and children born after who are not. The Court in arriving at this conclusion said : " The effect of the law is to give exemption from the operation of native law, as known and administered in the Colony of Natal, and not to give the exempted native the full status or rights of a European subject. . . . The exempted native is still subject to the special laws which apply only to natives and are not part of what is called native law. The exempted native is still disentitled to use the electoral franchise just as much as the unexempted native is ; he is not allowed to carry firearms or to obtain ammunition ; he is not allowed to obtain liquor. For exemption from these and other laws to which we have already alluded, it is still necessary for him to be relieved either by enactment or by the special authority of the Governor of the Colony ; and whenever exemption from the provisions of these special laws is granted it is always an exemption which applies only to an individual and not to members of the family " (pp. 315, 316). " The exempted natives feel very strongly the position in which children born subsequent to their parents' letters have been placed by recent decisions of the Court, and there is much force in their plea for uniformity in the family " (Natal Native Affairs Commission Report, p. 21). The same would seem to be true of the Orange River Colony and the Transvaal. It is also to be noted that the effect of exemption is not the same in all the colonies (The Native Affairs Commission, Appendix A-A 3).

There are other classes whose positions are peculiar :

§ 4. BASTARDS OR HALF-CASTES

The position of " bastards " or " half-castes " is very

uncertain. They have been held to be within the term
" native" in sect. 2 of Bechuanaland Proclamation 64 of
1869, as amended by Proclamation 113 of 1881 (Rex *v.*
Stern, 20 S.C. 564) ; a decision confirmed by the Court of
Appeal in a case (Superintendent of Police *v.* Alfred) the
facts of which were these : A Basuto woman who was the
wife of a French creole from Mauritius, though she assumed
on marriage the status of her husband, was held to be a
native within the Liquor Act (sect. 4, Act No. 38, 1896;
Natal, 27 L.R. 368). The Court admitted that, generally
speaking, the status of the husband becomes that of the
wife. But the definition in the statute was conclusive.
Altogether, the position of such persons is, as the Natal
Native Affairs Commission points out, peculiarly deplorable. They are outside the pale of tribal influences ;
they are not brought within the white community. Yet,
" as a rule, they are monogamists, and conform their lives
to civilised usages, and their aspirations, notwithstanding
many drawbacks, are impressively towards the legal
position of their ' white father,' objecting to being thrust
down to the level of their ' black mother ' " (p. 20); they
do not receive the status which, having regard to their
culture, they might fairly claim.

§ 5. ILLEGITIMATE CHILDREN

Their position may be illustrated by reference to an
actual case (Bewbew *v.* Dennis, 21 S.C.R. 139). The
plaintiff, a native woman of the Transkei Territory, had an
illegitimate child by the defendant, also a native. She
afterwards married another native. Her father gave the
custody of the child to the defendant, who paid for its
education. She sued the defendant for the delivery of the
child. The magistrate gave judgment for the defendant,
on the ground that "the native custom is very clear that
an unmarried native girl cannot claim any child she may

have had as hers. It is the property of her father." The
Acting Chief Magistrate dismissed the appeal. The
Supreme Court did the same (21 S.C.R. 139). "It is
proved," said the Court, "according to native law, that it
is not the mother of the illegitimate child who would be
entitled to the custody of the child, but it is the father· of
the mother who is entitled to the custody" (p. 141). It
may be mentioned that in Natal (Govu *v.* Stuart, 24 N.S.C.
440) it was held by the Supreme Court that the illegitimate child of a native woman by a European is a native
within sect. 5 of Act No. 49 of 1898 (overruling a contrary
decision in Strydom *v.* Sisila, "Farrer and Marwick's
Reports," 1901, p. 7). "The illegitimate son of a native
woman by a European father should be regarded as a
native for the purposes of this case" (p. 447).

It would seem advisable to lay down a uniform and
intelligible rule as to these cases.[1]

§ 6. OPERATION OF NATIVE LAW

Here, too, there has been no consistent policy. The
legislation on the subject seems fortuitous and fragmentary.
Each colony has gone its own way. Each colony has
from time to time altered its policy according to temporary
requirements. To understand the existing legislation that
of each colony must be studied.

As to Natal the policy of the Colony is described in the
case of Mahludi *v.* Rex (26 N.L.R. 298), in the judgment
of Bale, C.J. It appears that at one time there was a
hope that native law would die out, so that the natives
should come under European law. Only the process was
to be gradual. It was a principle in the proclamation of
Natal as a British colony that there was to be one law

---

[1] "The laws of the Transkeian Territory, so far as they affect natives,
are in a most anomalous condition" (Villiers, C.J., in Sekelini *v.* Sekelini, 21 S.C.R. p. 124).

for white and black. That has not come about, and is far distant.

In Natal there is a carefully prepared code of native law (Law No. 19, 1891) applicable to "any member of the aboriginal races or tribes of Africa south of the Equator."

By sect. 80 of Act No. 49 of 1898, "all civil native' cases shall be tried according to Native laws, customs, and usages, save so far as may be otherwise specially provided by law, or as may be of a nature to work some manifest injustice, or be repugnant to the settled principles and policy of natural equity."

In Cape Colony the native law is not codified. The native Courts have, as a rule, exclusive jurisdiction. The governing principle is that no Court has jurisdiction to try and decide disputes between native aborigines according to native law and custom, except where it is specially ordered (Tabata v. Tabata, 5 S.C. 328).[1] A suit to which a European is a party must be dealt with in the Ordinary courts in the ordinary way (M'Sindo v. Moriarty, 16 S.C. 539; Proclamation 110 of 1879).

In the Transkei native law, which is not codified, is partly applied to cases between natives. The Courts of Resident Magistrates have unlimited jurisdiction to try actions for damages. For the Transkei there is a Penal Code based mainly upon the criminal law of Cape Colony modified to meet local circumstances. As to the state of things in the Transkei we may quote the words of a judge: "The conflict of laws leads to a great deal of difficulty in dealing with questions arising in the Transkei, and it is really time this chaotic state of affairs should be removed" (Buchanan, J., 23 S.C.R. p. 564).

In Basutoland native law is applied to cases between natives.

---

[1] It is sometimes extremely difficult to say what is a native case. See, for example, Klaas v. Rex, 23 N.R., p. 12.

§ 7. Special Legislation as to Natives

There is a very large and highly complex mass of legislation in each colony specially affecting natives. For a trained lawyer to thread his way through it is not easy. For natives to be familiar with the laws which they are expected to obey is out of the question. We might deal with several aspects of the special legislation, if space permitted. We deal only with one or two, and first the law relative to marriage.

(a) Marriage

As to this institution, in regard to which it is pre-eminently desirable that there should be clear and simple legislation, there is confusion and uncertainty. This is true more or less of all the colonies. To take first the case of Cape Colony, the Courts have drawn attention to a strange omission. Act No. 16 of 1860 made provision for the appointment of marriage officers for solemnising the marriage of Mahommedans according to the Mahommedan customs and usages. It made no provision for marriages according to native customs and usages. In a case before the Courts the plaintiff summoned the defendant to return to him six head of cattle or their value, £20. The plaintiff, a Tembu, alleged that he took to wife a daughter of the defendant, also a Tembu, according to Tembu law and custom, and gave the defendant six head of cattle as dowry. The wife deserted the plaintiff without just cause, and by reason of this desertion he was entitled to recover the dowry. The defendant took exception to the summons that the contract of marriage according to the Tembu law was an immoral one and void; and that no action could be brought upon it. The Chief Justice, after pointing out that the Dutch law of marriage did not insist upon religious ceremony, remarked that "since the promulgation of the Act No. 16

of 1860, etc., the publication of banns, or its equivalent, has been deemed necessary, whether the marriage takes place before a minister of religion or before a lay marriage officer, except where a special licence has been granted. . . . The only mode in which a valid marriage can be contracted between natives in this Colony is before a minister of religion, or a lay marriage officer, with previous publication of banns or notice, or, failing these, by special licence. A union, therefore, founded only upon native usages and customs within the Colony proper is not a marriage, whatever rights may by special legislation have been given to the offspring of such a union in respect of distribution of property left by their parents upon their death. In the absence of special legislation recognising such a union as a valid marriage, Courts of law are bound—however much they may regret it—to treat the intercourse, I will not say as immoral, but as illicit " (Ngquobela v. Sihele, 10 S.C.R. pp. 351, 352). "Neither the Courts of the Colony (Cape) nor those of Tembuland can recognise as valid any marriage celebrated after the date of the Proclamation (1885) with a man who had one or more wives living at the time" (10 S.C.R. p. 357). And yet we find the same Court laying down principles as to Southern Rhodesia not easily reconcilable with the above. We may refer, for example, to the case of Rex v. Mawabe (20 S.C.R. 647), an appeal from Rhodesia. In a trial for murder it appeared that the accused, a native of Matabeleland, had two wives. One of them was adduced as witness for the prosecution. Objection was taken that her evidence was not admissible, she being the lawful wife of the accused. The Judge of First Instance overruled the objection. The Supreme Court upheld it. " I think," said the Chief Justice, " that we must hold that the marriage is legal. If it was legal, notwithstanding its polygamous nature, then it can only be because of native customs being introduced, and if native customs recognise polygamous marriages I do not see why these customs should not be evidence, unless they are contrary to natural law " (p. 649).

Under the present marriage law, or absence of it, serious practical difficulties may arise, and have arisen, as to whether particular persons are natives or Europeans. To illustrate this we would quote from the judgment in Reg *v.* Parrott (16 S.C. 452): " I fear the time will come when it will be impossible to decide whether particular persons are natives in terms of the Act in question (Act 28 of 1898). Natives to whom the definition applies are continually marrying or cohabiting with other members, and even Europeans, and in many cases it is difficult to say whether the progeny falls under the one class or the other." " Where a European is married to a native woman their children would probably not be treated as natives, but the illegitimate children of a native woman by a European, if retaining the features or the characteristics of the mother would be natives." " Nor can reliance be placed upon the fact that a person, to all appearance a native, bears a European name. Nothing is more common in this Colony than for natives to assume the names of Europeans whom they have served or who are well known to them " (p. 454).

In the Transkei and Basutoland the position seems to be this : marriages are valid (*a*) if celebrated by a minister of the Church of England according to its rites ; (*b*) if celebrated by a civil marriage officer duly appointed ; (*c*) if celebrated according to ordinary Kafir or Fingo forms, provided they are registered within three months.

On the other hand, in Natal a marriage is valid if entered into in accordance with native law and custom (Code, sect. 146).

In the Transvaal, ministers of coloured persons, having

the right to solemnise marriage, may now do so on compliance with certain conditions. But prior to the passing of Law No. 3 of 1897 (altered by Ordinance No. 29 of 1903), there was apparently no recognition by the State of the marriage of coloured persons. We may mention one decision of interest (Camel *v.* Dlamini, 1903, Transvaal 258). Two coloured persons who in 1895 went through the ceremony of marriage in the Wesleyan Church before a coloured minister, and who lived together as man and wife, were held not to be married. The marriage could not be made valid by Ordinance No. 29 of 1903, which declared such marriages valid provided they were registered with the appointed officer; it applied only to marriages by a minister " authorised to solemnise marriages," that is, ministers authorised by the Executive Government.

In the Orange River Colony marriage by native custom is (subject to certain qualifications) not recognised by law.

Obviously the state of things thus briefly described is unsatisfactory. Questioned as to this point, one of the witnesses before the Native Affairs Commission replied as follows: Q. " Don't you think it lowers the standard of the general morals of these people by the law not recognising their marriages?—A. I think it is a very great hardship." He added, " I don't think it is fair."

(*b*) *Succession*

As to this matter the Colonies have acted somewhat alike. The whole family system of all natives being dissimilar to that of Europe, it might be quite inequitable to apply the Roman-Dutch law, which equally divides the estate of the deceased among his children. Yet there was originally no jurisdiction to decide cases in Cape Colony according to native law and custom. Before 1864 all questions, including succession, were decided according to the common law of the Colony (Tabata *v.* Tabata, 5 S.C.R. 328). This was found to be unjust.

In Cape Colony, Natal, and the Transvaal, the estates of certain deceased natives are now administered, and their devolution determined, by native law. The first statute to this effect was the Native Succession Act, No. 18 of 1864, which declares that succession of natives holding certificates of citizenship [1] is to be determined by native law. Property left by an aboriginal native holding a certificate of citizenship is to be administered according to the usage of the tribe to which he belongs (s. 2). All controversies are to be decided according to native law by the Resident Magistrates of the district in which the deceased was domiciled (s. 3). A native may make a will according to colonial law. Land which he has purchased, and which he owns in his own right, he can dispose of by will. But in such case the administration of his estate takes place wholly according to colonial law (Sigidi's Exors. *v.* Matumba, 16 S.C. 497). It should be added as to Cape Colony that if a native who is a registered voter dies, his estate is administered as if he were a European (Act No. 39 of 1887, s. 1).

§ 8. Defects of Present Law

We have stated enough to show that there is need of some general action in regard to the status of natives. One of the first results of federation will be, it may be hoped, to put an end to, or diminish, this diversity. The variety of the law applicable to natives is great. So is its uncertainty. The recent Natal Native Affairs Commission remarks that "in the case of natives the civil rights they enjoy, and which have been confirmed to them by law, compare very favourably with those possessed by Europeans" (p. 12). None the less is it true that the law leaves the

[1] Act No. 17 of 1864.

position of many persons undefined. It places in the position of the raw Kafir persons who are much more in sympathy with the whites. It casts a slur on marriages which, according to popular opinion, are valid. Law might be made a great instrument of education ; a means of helping to bring about some clear approximation between races. It is questionable whether this opportunity has been so used. It is a serious defect in any body of laws that they are out of touch or harmony with the sentiments of any considerable portion of the community in which they are applied. It is a still greater defect that they are not completely in touch or harmony with the sentiments of any part of the community. This is not necessarily a reproach to the Governments concerned ; these defects may be to some extent inevitable where people once living under a tribal system of personal rule come under a Government of the modern type. But there is force in the observation of the Natal Commissioners : "We never stopped to think that our system had become too impersonal for the masses, or to see the pathos in a simple people looking for fatherly advice and assistance from a purely judicial officer, or longing to consult an exalted and virtually inaccessible Minister" (p. 12). "It is apparent to all who understand the situation that the natives are being over-administered, and that they are ignorant of many of the laws which affect themselves" (p. 13).

CHAPTER VI

EDUCATION[1]

§ 1. INTRODUCTORY

THE educational work which the missionaries of many churches and societies have been carrying on among the natives has not yet received the attention and support in South Africa which it deserves, but its value has at least been recognised both by the Imperial and the Colonial Governments. The natives also are showing a keen appreciation of its benefits, and are contributing substantially to its maintenance. Public sentiment on the question is, moreover, slowly changing in favour of a more progressive policy. The old controversies as to the wisdom of providing education for natives have now given place to the practical problem of ascertaining what form of

[1] The statements contained in this chapter are mainly derived from the following sources: The Annual Reports of the Education and Native Affairs Departments of the various colonies; The Annual Colonial Reports on Basutoland and the Bechuanaland Protectorate; The Annual Reports of the British South Africa Company; Special Reports of the Board of Education on Educational Subjects, vol. 13 (Cd. 2378); Mr. E. B. Sargant's Preliminary Report to the High Commissioner on Native Education, and his Report on Education in Basutoland, 1905-6; Evidence of witnesses before the South African Native Affairs Commission, 1903-5; The Duff Missionary Lectures for 1902, by Dr. James Stewart, published under the title of "Dawn in the Dark Continent" (Oliphant, Anderson and Ferrier); Dr. Theal's "History of South Africa"; "History of the Wesleyan Methodist Church of South Africa" by the Rev. J. Whiteside (Elliot Stock); Articles on Educational subjects in the Lovedale magazine, *The Christian Express*; and information supplied by various correspondents and informants of the Committee.

education is likely to produce the best results. It is clear that the education required by natives is not in all respects identical with that needed by Europeans. The moral standards and new ideas which it is the object of the native schools to inculcate have to be grafted on to the stock of tribal tradition and sentiment; and the character of the instruction to be given in these schools must also to some extent be determined by the probable future position of the scholars. Educational policy is thus intimately bound up with the transition from tribal custom to civilised law now taking place among the native peoples of South Africa, and must be considered with constant reference to the new and changing conditions which that transition is creating. This point of the problem has been justly emphasised by Mr. Sargant in his instructive preliminary report to the High Commissioner. " Law," he points out, " is one of the chief factors in determining a system of education, while education is one of the chief factors in producing a change of law." And he proceeds to show that " while, as a consequence of the immense divergence between many of the laws necessary for the good government of the two races (*i.e.* whites and natives), separate educational schemes are also required, care must be taken so to trace the lines of the scheme of education appropriate to the more backward race that it shall in time produce that change of law which is required for a closer approximation and understanding between the black man and the white."

This definition of the function of native education deserves the closest attention ; it supplies the standard by which the various educational systems which have grown up in the South African colonies will sooner or later have to be tested. These systems have been established, somewhat fortuitously, by a number of agencies, working on different lines and under a great variety of

local conditions ; and in the following pages we shall
endeavour, first, to trace briefly the progress of their work,
and then to consider, in the light of recent investigations,
how far that work has been justified by its results, and in
what respects changes of method have become desirable.

As the conditions under which the educational work
among the natives has been carried on vary considerably
in the different colonies, it seems advisable for the sake of
clearness to deal separately with the progress of this
work in each colony.

§ 2. CAPE COLONY

To trace the origin of native education in Cape Colony
it is necessary to go back to the middle of the seventeenth
century.   In 1656, or about four years after the first
Dutch settlement at the Cape, a school was established for
slave children and Hottentots. This school was only carried
on for a month or two, but it was reopened in 1661, and
then lasted somewhat longer.   Another school was opened
in 1663 for Europeans, Hottentots, and slave children ;
and in 1676 a school was established for coloured children
only.   In 1779 about 700 white and coloured children seem
to have been receiving education in the Cape Town district,
and soon after that date the influence of Dr. Van Lier and
his Lutheran congregation at Cape Town, and the arrival
of missionaries from Europe, gave a new impetus to educational work.   The first Moravian missionary, George
Schmidt, had opened a school for Hottentots at Baviaans
Kloof (Valley of Baboons), about seventy miles from Cape
Town, in 1737, but after carrying on his work for about
six years he was prohibited by the Government from
administering the rite of baptism to his converts, and
thereupon returned to Europe.   More tolerant views,
however, gradually prevailed, and in 1792 the Moravians

were able to send out three missionaries, who re-established
the mission at Baviaans Kloof.   In spite of constant
difficulties, their work prospered.   Baviaans Kloof, re-
named Genadendal (Valley of Grace) in 1806, grew into
a well-ordered village, with a school destined to become
an important educational institution ; new stations were
opened ; and the Cape Government assisted the brother-
hood by grants of money and land.

The Moravians were soon followed by missionaries of
other societies.   In 1799 the London Missionary Society
sent out Dr. Vanderkemp, who laboured among the
Hottentots and founded the mission station of Bethels-
dorp.   Other missions were carried on by this Society
on the Orange River and elsewhere, and between 1820 and
1850 it established its important work in Bechuanaland,
especially associated with the names of Moffat, Livingstone,
and Mackenzie.   This Society has played a notable and
sometimes stormy part in the history of South Africa.
Under the guidance of Dr. Philip, it became involved in
frequent controversies with the colonists ; but it has done
much to instil confidence in the justice of British rule
among the natives, and to win public recognition of their
rights to equitable treatment. . To its missionaries, Moffat
and Ashton, the Bechuanas owe their translation of the
Bible.

This adventurous and energetic society was followed
in 1821 by the Glasgow Missionary Society (afterwards
amalgamated with the Free Church of Scotland), who in
that year established a mission on the Tyumie River in
Kaffraria.   This mission was the origin of the well-known
Lovedale Institution, and it proved to be the forerunner of
a number of Scottish Presbyterian missions in Kaffraria
and the Transkei.   The Scottish Presbyterian missionaries
have laid special stress on the importance of combining
educational with evangelistic work.   Under the able

guidance of Dr. James Stewart, the Lovedale Missionary
Institution, opened in 1841, became the leading educational centre for natives in South Africa; and a similar
institution was subsequently established by the Free
Church at Blythswood, towards the building of which the
natives themselves contributed no less than £4,500. The
United Free Church also have an industrial school for
native girls at Emgwali.

Almost simultaneously with the establishment of the
first Presbyterian mission, the Society for the Propagation
of the Gospel initiated the mission work of the Church of
England in the Colony. For some years the Society made
slow progress, but in 1847 new life was infused into its
efforts by the consecration of Dr. Gray as the first bishop
of Cape Town. Under his vigorous administration the
work of the Anglican Church grew rapidly. The dioceses
of Grahamstown and Natal were added to that of Cape
Town in 1853, the Orange Free State (now Bloemfontein)
in 1863, Zululand in 1870, St. John's (after Dr. Gray's
death) in 1873, Pretoria in 1878, Mashonaland in 1891,
and Lebombo in 1893. These nine dioceses, with that
of St. Helena, now constitute the Province of South
Africa, of which the Archbishop of Cape Town is the
metropolitan. The religious and educational work among
the natives which Dr. Gray instituted has been carried on
by other missionary bishops, notably by Dr. Callaway, the
first bishop of St. John's, well known as a Zulu and Kafir
scholar, and his successor, Dr. Key. The important
Zonnebloem College for the sons of chiefs is one of the
chief results of Dr. Gray's interest in native education, and
in founding this institution he had the warm support of the
Governor of the Colony, Sir George Grey. The Church
of England has also established several valuable educational institutions, at which native teachers are trained and
industrial instruction is provided, the most successful being

those at Keiskama Hoek and Grahamstown; and it is carrying on a number of elementary schools.

Before the arrival at the Cape of the first Church of England and Presbyterian missionaries the Wesleyan Methodist Missionary Society had established a mission in Little Namaqualand in 1816, under the charge of the Rev. B. Shaw. Seven years later the Rev. W. Shaw opened a mission at Wesleyville among the Gcalekas, and a number of other stations were subsequently established in Kaffraria. During the Kafir wars these stations had to be abandoned; but on the restoration of peace they were reopened, and the work of the Wesleyan missionaries extended rapidly. Schools were established at Grahamstown and Kamastone, and industrial schools at Salem, Peddie, Lesseyton, and Healdtown. Of these the most important was the school at Healdtown. Sir George Grey personally selected the site, and the Imperial Government made a grant of £3,000 towards the cost of the buildings Unfortunately, after Sir George Grey left South Africa, the industrial training given at these schools was discontinued in consequence of the withdrawal of the Government grants. The day school at Healdtown, however, was still carried on, and a new department was subsequently added for training native teachers and ministers. The theological class was removed to Lesseyton in 1880, but the classes for teachers, which have been unusually successful, have become a special feature of the Healdtown institution. The Wesleyans have also established training schools at Clarkebury, Bensonvale, and Buntingville, and, for girls, at Shawbury; and they provide industrial instruction at their schools at Clarkebury, Bensonvale, Butterworth, and Osborne, and in the Ayliff Institution for girls at Peddie. Besides these institutions, they have a large number of day-schools in connection with their numerous mission stations. The missions of the Wesleyan

Missionary Society in Cape Colony, Natal, and the Orange
River Colony have now been placed under the control of
a South African Conference. The work of the Society
is primarily evangelistic, but during the last thirty years
it has given much attention to native education. One of
its missionaries, the Rev. W. Boyce, produced the first
Kafir grammar ; and another, the Rev. W. Appleyard, was
the author of a later and more complete grammar, and
was also the translator of the first complete Kafir Bible.

During recent years the Dutch Reformed Church, under
the influence of the Murrays and others, has begun to take
an active part in mission work, especially among the
coloured people in the Colony, and it is now carrying on
a number of schools for the coloured children. Schools for
coloured and native children have also been opened by the
Roman Catholics and Lutherans, the Rhenish, Berlin, and
Paris Evangelical Missionary Societies, and others, including
several native churches or organisations. But the educational work of these churches and societies is on a much
smaller scale than that of the United Free Church of
Scotland, the Church of England, and the Wesleyans.

In spite of the influence of Sir George Grey and other
Governors, and of many leading colonists, there has always
been a persistent, though steadily weakening, opposition
to the efforts of the missionaries to improve the condition and status of the natives. Nevertheless, in the matter of
native education Cape Colony has hitherto been by far the
most progressive of the self-governing colonies in South
Africa. There is, it is true, only one Government
school for natives, which was established under exceptional circumstances near Maitland. But since about 1841
the Government has given systematic support to the
educational work among the natives, and many of the
schools carried on under recognised Christian denominations
are now receiving grants-in-aid, and have become subject

to the regulations and inspection of the Education Department. This policy of aiding, but not undertaking direct responsibility for, native schools was in the main adhered to in the School Board Act of 1905. The status of the voluntary schools for natives remains undisturbed by that Act; but it contains certain provisions enabling the Education Department, in conjunction with the school board of any district, to establish a public undenominational school for the children " of people of other than European parentage or extraction," if at least fifty parents of such children in the district petition for it. If there is sufficient accommodation at a school of this kind for the children of non-European extraction, the school board is empowered, after obtaining the approval of a majority of the ratepayers and of the committee of the school, to make the attendance of these children compulsory.

According to the report of Dr. Muir, the Superintendent-General of Education, for 1905–6, there were at the end of that year 720 aided " mission schools " in the Colony proper, and 745 aided " aborigines' schools " in the Transkeian Territories for coloured and native children, with a total enrolment of 51,054 boys and 51,795 girls. A comparison of these figures with the corresponding statistics for 1898 shows during these eight years an increase of 135 in the number of mission schools, and of 271 in the number of aborigines' schools, and an addition to the enrolment of no less than 11,075 boys and 12,025 girls. The attainments of the children show that there has also been an improvement in the efficiency of the schools, although 62·51 per cent. of the children in the mission schools, and 55·96 per cent. of those in the aborigines' schools in 1906 were still under Standard I.

Dr. Muir, in his report for 1903–4, drew attention to the fact that better results are obtained by the aborigines' schools of the Transkeian Territories than by the mission

schools of the Colony proper ; and he attributed this difference mainly to the existence of institutions in the east
of the Colony known as "aborigines' training schools," in
which teachers are trained for the aborigines' schools. The
paucity of training schools appears to be one of the most
serious defects in the Cape Colony system of native
education. In 1906 only eleven such schools (with 715
pupils) were mentioned in the report of the Superintendent-
General ; and in view of the good work which they
accomplish, it is much to be regretted that there had been
no increase in their number since 1898. The fact that
only 859 of the 2,843 teachers in the aided mission and
aborigines' schools in 1906 held certificates shows how
great is the need of institutions of this kind.

It is satisfactory to note that there has of late been
a substantial increase in the amount of the Government
grant. In 1898 the grant for mission and aborigines'
schools (including training schools) was £46,665 as against
a local contribution of £24,098 ; in 1905–6 it had risen
to £74,132 as against a local contribution of £44,040. The
grant in respect of each pupil present at inspection in the
latter year was at the rate of 16s. 2d. for mission schools,
15s. 1d. for aborigines' schools, and £8 17s. 5d. for
aborigines' training schools. The grants to mission and
aborigines' schools are still, however, on a much lower scale
than the grants made to schools for white children, the
corresponding rate of grant to a third-class public school
in 1905–6 being £2 9s. 4d. On the other hand, in the
case of native schools the Government grants bear a
higher proportion to the local contribution than in the
case of schools for whites, and the requirements of the
Education Department with regard to the qualification of
teachers and equipment are less stringent.

During the last few years a number of schools have been
opened by natives and coloured people independently of

the white churches or missionaries. The Order of Ethiopia
and the native church known as the Presbyterian Church of
Africa have succeeded in obtaining State aid for some of
their schools, and both these bodies are apparently doing
useful educational work. The African Methodist Episcopal
Church has opened a large school, the Bethel Institute, in
Cape Town, with about four hundred students, and several
mission schools in various parts of the Colony ; but apparently none of these schools have received Government
grants, although, presumably, the Education Department
would not withhold grants from them if they complied
with its regulations and were not injuring other schools.[1]

At Lovedale a few white scholars are educated side by side
with the native children, and there are a few white children
at the Zonnebloem College and in some of the mission
schools. But as a general rule white and native children
are educated separately, and in most cases this is probably
the wiser method. Dr. Muir draws attention to the good
feeling shown by the natives at Cape Town in acquiescing
in this arrangement. He states that he has never had one
really serious case of a conflict between coloured and white
parents, and that natives do not press unreasonably for
the admission of their children to the white schools.

The children in the mission and aborigines' schools are
usually only educated up to Standard IV., and the
Education Department does not encourage these schools
to attempt to give general instruction in higher standards.
This means that the ordinary education given in these
schools includes little except reading and writing, and arithmetic up to calculations with money and ordinary weights
and measures, and South African geography. An exception,
however, is made in favour of pupil teachers, who have to
reach Standard VI. in order to enter the special training

[1] For further particulars of educational work carried on by natives,
see Chapter VII.

institutions.   The curriculum in these schools is much the same as in the schools for white children, and English is used as the medium of instruction in all the standards. Industrial training of various kinds is given to boys and girls at Lovedale [1] and Blythswood, and at the Church of England school at Grahamstown, to boys only at the Church of England schools at Umtata, at the Wesleyan schools at Clarkebury, Butterworth, Bensonvale, and Osborn, and at the London Missionary Society's school at Vryburg, and to girls only at the Church of England schools at Cape Town and Port Elizabeth, the United Free Church school at Emgwali, the Wesleyan school at Peddie, and the Roman Catholic school at Wynberg. But in September 1906 there were only 268 boys and 290 girls receiving industrial training at these schools; and this side of the educational work in the Colony clearly calls for more attention than it has hitherto received. The Education Department, however, is encouraging industrial instruction by making apprentice grants and contributing to teachers' salaries, and Dr. Muir particularly desired to introduce the teaching of gardening in all schools where the necessary land is available.

Most of the mission and aborigines' schools have native teachers.   These teachers are often insufficiently trained, and are not always successful in maintaining discipline ; but on the whole they seem to do their work fairly well, and many of them have a good influence on their scholars. As a rule, they do not show much enthusiasm for industrial education. This may partly be due to the defective training which most of them have received.

The Government has given no grants for the provision of higher education for natives, except in connection with

---

[1] For particulars of the system of education adopted at Lovedale see this Committee's previous volume, " The Natives of South Africa " (John Murray), p. 184 et seq.

the training of teachers ; and the facilities which at present
exist for such education are fast becoming inadequate.
At the Lovedale Institution pupils are educated up to
Standard VI., from which they can pass into the normal
department for the training of teachers, or take a course
to prepare them for the school higher, or matriculation,
examinations ; and there is also a theological course for the
training of ministers. But during the ten years between
1891 and 1901 only eighteen natives entered the matriculation class and only seventy-five the school higher classes,
and in 1907 out of sixty-four native students in the
" college " department only seven were in the matriculation
class. There were, however, about a hundred and fifty
students in the normal department. Higher education can
also be obtained by natives at the Zonnebloem College,
where the students, after passing Standard VI., can take
up the course for teachers or enter a matriculation
class. Very few Zonnebloem boys, however, have passed
the matriculation examination, and the Warden informed
the Native Affairs Commission that none of his pupils
had done so during the preceding three years. With
these exceptions, there seem to be no institutions in the
Colony at which natives can obtain higher education, unless
they wish to be trained as teachers ; and it is therefore
sometimes extremely difficult for the native who is in a
position to give his children a good education to find a
satisfactory and convenient school to which to send them.
Not long ago Mr. Tengo Jabavu, the editor of the " *Imvo*,"
reluctantly sent his son to England for education, because
he was not allowed to enter Dale College or any other
college in the Colony receiving the higher Government
grants ; and a number of natives have recently been sent
for education to negro institutions in the United States.
In view of the desire of an increasing number of natives
for higher education, and of their willingness to contribute

substantially towards its cost, it seems clear that the time
has come when the Government should give its support to
some institution for supplying their needs in this respect.

It is estimated that the average cost of educating a boy
at Lovedale is about £20 a year, exclusive of rent. The
pupils or their parents pay fees varying from £12 to £22
per annum, and the balance of the cost is provided by the
Government grant and the subsidy from the United Free
Church. At the Zonnebloem College the cost of each pupil
is about the same ; the fees from each student amount to
about £16 per annum, and the balance is met by the
endowment and the Government grant. In the case of
an ordinary mission school the Government grant is at the
rate of £1 for every 10s. contributed from local sources.

In part of the Transkeian Territories contributions
towards the salaries of teachers in the aborigines' schools
have been paid through the headmen, but a much more
satisfactory arrangement has been adopted in the districts
in which the local government clauses of the Glen Grey
Act are in force. In these districts an education rate is
levied by the district council, and the proceeds are handed
over to the General Transkeian Council. The General
Council then applies this money in making grants towards
the salaries of the teachers in the districts in which it has
been collected. The General Council also contributes
towards the expenses for school furniture and other educational purposes. The district councils have sometimes
been remiss in collecting the rate, but on the whole the
system seems to have worked well, and the schools in
these districts are in a far better financial position than the
mission schools in which the salary of a teacher depends
on the qualifications of his pupils and is subject to
considerable variations. Dr. Muir stated before the Native
Affairs Commission that in some cases the General Council
contributed very nearly as much as the Government, and

that its payments were made regularly. " In those districts," he informed the Commissioners, "where the Glen Grey Act has been proclaimed better teachers are got, schools are in better condition generally, and the people take a good deal more interest in education. Had I my wish, I should have these clauses of the Glen Grey Act proclaimed everywhere throughout the Territories."

§ 3. NATAL

The first schools for natives in Natal were opened in 1836 on the Umlazi by Congregationalist missionaries sent out by the American Board of Missions. After eight or nine years the war between the Boers and the Zulus compelled them to abandon their station, but one of their number, Dr. Adams, subsequently returned to it, and after Natal became a British colony the American Zulu Mission, as it is now called, grew and flourished. It has now many stations and out-stations in the Colony, and has established a number of schools, of which the chief are its institution at Amanzimtote, which includes a theological school, and a girls' school at Inanda. A Zulu dictionary and grammar have been prepared and the Bible translated by missionaries of this society.

Many schools for natives have also been established by the Wesleyans, the United Free Church of Scotland, the Church of England, and the Roman Catholics, and by other churches and societies of various nationalities. It has, however, been extremely difficult in this colony to overcome the widespread prejudice against the education of natives ; and, although the Government now recognises and assists the efforts of the missionaries and others to carry on native schools, the colonists generally have shown little sympathy with the work. The lack of public support is no doubt primarily due to a certain feeling of anxiety arising

from the overwhelming number of the natives. This feeling
has been aggravated by the proximity to the towns of
large masses of tribal natives, who have settled in locations
in the centre of the Colony without any buffer of partially
civilised natives, as in Cape Colony, between them and
the whites. The colonists are thus brought into constant
contact with raw tribal natives. They have, perhaps
naturally, insisted on the maintenance of a rigorous colour
line, and have become extremely jealous of anything that
tends towards racial equality. In Cape Colony the even
balance of political parties has led to the concession of
privileges to natives in order to obtain the support of the
native electorate. But this motive does not operate in
Natal, where the Dutch element is comparatively weak, and
only two natives have succeeded in obtaining the franchise.
These circumstances may well account for the unprogressive native policy of the Colony. It is a question
whether the whites in Natal would not have been in
a more satisfactory position had they shown more
sympathy with native sentiment, and taken more active
steps to evoke native loyalty. Particularly is this the
case with regard to the question of education ; for the
desire of the natives for education merits encouragement
rather than repression, and it offers the Government an
exceptional opportunity for promoting better relations
between the two races. The natives are said to complain
that the Government takes little interest in them, except
with regard to the payment of taxes, and that it gives
money grudgingly for their benefit. Assistance in providing schools would remove a genuine grievance, and
would be greatly appreciated, at any rate by the natives
who have come under the influence of the missions.[1]

The Government of Natal has for some time past
recognised the reasonableness of the natives' demand for

[1] Known as the Amakola natives.

education, although it has only seen its way to take somewhat hesitating and tentative measures to encourage the
educational work. It began to deal with the question in
something like a systematic way in 1884, and in 1886
a Government industrial school was established at the
Zwaartkop location. This school, however, proved a
failure, and was closed in 1891. Two Government schools
for "coloured" children have now been opened, but all
schools for natives are carried on by religious bodies of
various nationalities, or, in a few cases, by private persons,
the Government contributing small grants-in-aid.

In 1905-6 165 schools for natives were receiving
Government grants, and these schools had a total average
enrolment of 4,256 boys and 6,815 girls, with 91 European
and 244 native teachers. Ten of these schools had ceased
to work at the end of the year. The remaining 155 included 16 boarding-schools, 127 day-schools, and 12 schools
with both boarders and day scholars. The two Government schools for coloured children had an average
enrolment of 98 boys and 92 girls; and there were 15
"coloured" schools, with 266 boys and 187 girls receiving
Government grants. It is disappointing to find that there
were fewer aided schools for natives in 1906 than in 1899,
when the number of such schools was 188. This decrease
appears to be mainly due to the Education Department
having required higher qualifications from the teachers
than in previous years—a change of policy which led to
the closing of 54 schools in one year. The action of the
Department may have tended to raise the standard of
efficiency, but the closing of so many schools shows
how great is the need of further provision for the
training of teachers.

In districts outside the effective influence of the missionaries the natives are apathetic about the education of
their children ; and in some parts of the Colony chiefs have

objected to the teaching of Christianity, and have discouraged their people from sending children to the mission
schools. It is to be feared also that some of the magistrates take little interest in educational progress. On the
other hand, the Christianised natives are eager for instruction, and in some cases they have established schools on
their own responsibility. They have, however, found it
difficult to raise funds for the teachers' salaries, and
hitherto the Education Department has refused to give
them any assistance.

As in Cape Colony, there has of late been an increase in
the amount of the Government grants, which rose from
£5,658 in 1899 to £7,042 in 1905–6. The rate of the
grant also increased from 14s. 1d. per child in average
attendance in 1899 to 17s. 11d. per child in 1905–6. Nevertheless, the rate is still on a very low scale as compared
with the £6 8s. 7d. granted per child in the white schools,
and the total Government expenditure on native education in the year 1905-6 (excluding the upkeep of the
Education Office) only amounted to £8,227, a sum which
bears no adequate proportion to the educational needs of
the natives or to their contributions to the revenue.

It has in the past been the practice of the Education
Department only to allow aided schools to give instruction
up to Standard IV., except in training teachers. The
recognised curriculum includes reading, writing, arithmetic, geography, a little history, and instruction in knowledge of common things. Special stress is laid on the
speaking of English, but the native language is used as
the medium of instruction in the lower standards. In the
better schools the Department requires manual work. As
a rule this merely means instruction in agriculture, but in
some of the schools boys are taught leather work, advanced horticulture, stone work, waggon-making and other
trades. The girls are taught knitting, crotchet, and sewing

in the day-schools, and in the boarding-schools sewing,
fancy needlework, cooking, laundry, house, garden, and
field work.   Most of the day-schools are held, at great
inconvenience, in places of worship,[1] but in spite of many
difficulties there seems to have been a steady improvement
during the last few years in the attendance and morale of
the children.   They are stated to be "cleaner, more
obedient, and more intelligent," but comparatively few of
them reach the higher standards, the report of the
Superintendent-General for 1905–6 showing that in the
165 schools inspected during that year, no less than 8,119
pupils were under Standard II., 2,707 in Standards II.
to V., and only 245 above Standard V.   This unsatisfactory
result is probably due in large degree to the lack of
properly qualified native teachers.   Although some of the
boarding-schools have classes for student teachers, further
provision for their training seems to be urgently required.
The Education Department is, however, fully alive to this
need, and is taking steps to meet it ; and its report
shows that native teachers are gradually becoming
better qualified for their duties.

Good industrial training is given in the Trappist schools,
especially at Maria Ratschitz, and at the Adams's
Seminary, the Wesleyan school at Edendale, St. Augustine's
(Church of England) in Zululand, and in the girls'
schools at Inanda, Umzumbi and Indaleni ; and special
grants are made by the Government for this work.   The
Governor recently opened an industrial school under the
charge of a native, John Dube, at Ohlange.

It is estimated that the Government grants provide about
one half of the cost of carrying on the aided native schools.

[1] The Education Department has intimated that after July 1, 1908,
no school will receive a grant unless it is held in a building used
exclusively for educational purposes.   It is to be hoped that, if this
regulation is enforced, it will be accompanied by liberal building
grants.

In most of these schools small fees are charged and applied towards the payment of teachers' salaries. These fees vary from twopence to a shilling a month in day-schools and from £2 10s. to £8 per annum in boarding-schools. In unprogressive districts it is difficult, if not impossible, for missionaries to enforce the payments. In the diocese of Zululand, for instance, no fees appear to be charged, but the people contribute in church offertories, and sometimes subscribe towards church and school expenses. The churches and societies usually collect in this way such local contributions as they can, and provide the balance of the necessary funds themselves.

At present there is no special institution in the Colony for providing higher education for natives. A scheme for establishing an important educational institution at Watersmeet has, however, been under consideration. A body of natives offered land for this purpose, and labour and material "to the utmost of their power." The project has been approved by the Superintendent-General of Education, and a considerable sum has been placed on the estimates for building the proposed school-house, normal college and workshops for industrial training. Unfortunately, legal difficulties have arisen with regard to the site, and the scheme seems to be making little progress. But the interest which the Government has taken in this project shows an appreciation of the value of the educational work, which, in the past, it must be admitted, has been somewhat lacking.

The recent Natal Commission on Native Affairs strongly recommended that the Government should recognise and take advantage of the knowledge and experience of the missionaries in educational matters by constituting "a small Board of Advice, upon which all the denominations might be directly or indirectly represented," with the Superintendent of Education or the Senior Inspector as

chairman, to assist the Education Department "in
the settlement of general principles and broad rules."
The Commission also advised the establishment of small
industrial schools and of a central training institution for
teachers and industrial work, and that grants should be
given to existing schools on a more liberal scale and
under less stringent conditions.

§ 4. BASUTOLAND

The educational work among the Basuto has to a large
extent been in the hands of the missionaries of a single
organisation, the Paris Evangelical Mission Society. This
Society is specially representative of French Protestantism ;
but its missionaries, who have been men exceptionally
fitted for their work, have included Scottish Presbyterians
as well as French and Swiss Protestants. The Society has
concentrated much of its energies on its Basutoland
mission, which it has organised as a separate department ;
and it has been rewarded by the remarkable success of
this mission. The policy of the Society and its position
in the country have given the educational work in
Basutoland an unusual unity and completeness, which
make it peculiarly instructive as an illustration of the
effects of Christian training on a native people.

In Basutoland the educational movement also has a
special interest owing to the distinctive national character
which it has acquired from the close connection between
the work of the Paris Society and the fortunes of the
Basuto. When the pioneer missionaries of the Society,
MM. Casalis, Arbousset, and Gosselin, entered the
country in 1833, at the invitation of Moshesh, that able and
far-sighted chief was already engaged in the task of welding
together the scattered clans and tribes who, under his
astute leadership, ultimately became the Basuto nation. In

1831 he had succeeded in driving back from his fortress of Thaba Bosiu the dangerous hordes of Moselekatse; and in 1840 the collapse of the Zulu power under Dingan removed one of the most serious obstacles in his way. But on every side he was beset with dangers. His authority depended on the goodwill of his people; rival chiefs disputed his claims; and, notwithstanding his desire to maintain peaceful relations with the white colonists, the unruly acts of his followers involved him in disputes with the Governments of Cape Colony and the Orange Free State, which on several occasions led to serious fighting. Throughout the perilous years during which he was gradually consolidating and extending his power, the missionaries rendered him invaluable services. They became his trusted councillors; they assisted him in his negotiations with the Colonial Government; and they spared no efforts to promote friendly relations with the white colonists. More than once their influence and wise counsels saved him and his people from disaster. And, on his side, Moshesh from first to last gave them his loyal support. Although he never embraced Christianity, he was always their protector; he supplied missionaries with land; he directed his people to live near their churches and schools, and he even took part in their services. Under the shelter of his authority the work of the Society developed rapidly. Its stations and schools grew and multiplied; and wherever its representatives went they spread abroad a new spirit of progress and a new standard of life. The work of the mission was, however, greatly hindered by frequent fighting; and the missionaries shared the misfortunes of the Basuto. Once they were compelled entirely to abandon their missions. In 1865–6 the Government of the Orange Free State annexed a considerable portion of the country, containing ten of the twelve stations which the Society had established, and, notwithstanding

the protests of President Brand, the missionaries and their
families were expelled as partisans of the Basuto. The
station at Thaba Bosiu was destroyed, and the whole
mission was thus practically broken up. This unjustifiable
act roused a storm of indignation in England, and when
hostilities again broke out between the Free State and
the Basuto in 1867, the British Government decided to
intervene. The Basuto, as they desired, were in the
following year declared to be British subjects ; a considerable portion of the ceded territory was restored to them ;
and in 1871, the year after Moshesh's death, the country
was formally annexed to Cape Colony. On the restoration
of peace the missionaries resumed their work ; and,
although interrupted in 1880 by the Gun War, which led
to Basutoland being taken over by the Imperial Government, it has continued to make steady progress, and is
still one of the chief factors in promoting the peace and
well-being of the Basuto.

This close identification of the Paris Society with the
struggles and growth of the Basuto people and the
admirable work and wide-spread influence of its missionaries,
have given it a unique position in the country. Its
missionaries officiate at the obsequies of the paramount
chief; the church which it has established, "the Church
of Basutoland," has over 40,000 adherents ; and its schools
and training institutions practically constitute the national
system of education. The Resident Commissioners have
taken a lively interest in its work ; and, as the country
is strictly reserved for the Basuto, there has been an
absence of opposition arising from racial prejudices. Under
these exceptional conditions, the Society, notwithstanding
its lack of adequate funds, has been able to achieve
remarkable results, of which not the least important are
the effects of its educational work.

At the end of 1905 the Society had 185 schools registered

in the Government offices, and its scholars at the date
of the census of April 1904 numbered 11,939. Nearly all
the schools are elementary day-schools under native
teachers; but there is a higher industrial school for boys
at Leloaleng; an industrial and boarding-school for girls,
which has recently been removed from Thaba Bosiu to
Thabana Morena; a normal school for training teachers
at Morija; and a small theological college or school at
Thaba Bosiu, which was to be removed to Morija. The
Leloaleng school, which was opened about twenty-seven
years ago, has become an important institution with about
thirty scholars. Most of the pupils at this school are in
or over Standard IV., and they are generally not admitted
until they have passed Standard II. They now pay fees
amounting to £4 a year. They can take a three years'
course in masonry or carpentry, or a four years' course in
waggon-building and forge work; and the thorough
training they receive is having tangible results. "Besides
the buildings at Leloaleng itself and at Moyeni," writes
Mr. Sargant, "these apprentices have built the church
(P.E.M.S.) at Siloe, additions to the church (P.E.M.S.) at
Masitise, and some of the new buildings at Morija. To
this list may be added some of the buildings of the
Government Industrial School at Maseru. But the chief
part of their work has been done for natives themselves.
In many of the villages, cottages, not unlike those to be
found in Northumberland, are now built of prepared stone,
either smooth or bull-faced." The Leloaleng pupils have
vainly tried to obtain employment at Bloemfontein, where
a municipal by-law forbids the contractors to employ
native carpenters and builders for town work. But they
have found employment in East Griqualand and in
Basutoland itself; and it is noteworthy that most of them
hold land and cattle, and thus pursue their trades without
altogether abandoning their more natural pastoral life.

Good industrial and higher education is also given in the girls' school at Thabana Morena, and more advanced education is provided at the Morija school for training native teachers. The first station of the Society was established at Morija, which is still the headquarters of the Society's work ; and its normal school has made it an important educational centre. This institution, which was opened in 1868, shortly after the war with the Free State, had 134 students in 1905. It is divided into a preparatory school, in which instruction is given in Standards V. and VI., and the normal school proper, with a three years' course. The students do their own cooking, washing, mending of clothes, and similar work ; and they gain some knowledge of ·horticulture by working in the gardens of the missionaries. But they receive no systematic industrial training, and this omission has placed them at a dis-advantage when competing in the Cape Colony examina-tions. Another interesting institution is the Society's theological college or school at Thaba Bosiu. This institution, which is under the charge of M. Jacottet, is intended for the training of native ministers. The students, in 1905 four in number, are chosen with great care. Before they can be admitted, they must have worked in some mission as catechists or teachers, and they must also have been accepted as students by the Seboka or council of the Church of Basutoland. Each student has a separate house or apartments with a garden, and receives £15 a year for his expenses. If he is married, he brings his family with him. Small as this institution is, its importance is great, for the Paris Society entrusts its native ministers with extremely responsible duties, and a native minister, if well qualified for his post, has often remarkable influence over his fellow-natives.

Most of the elementary schools of the Society are in the south of the country, which has come more under the

influence of the missionaries than the north ; and in
progressive districts a large proportion of the pupils are
girls.   These schools often have to be held in the churches
of the mission—an arrangement which is not conducive
to the comfort of teachers or scholars—and they frequently
lack proper furniture and equipment.   The teachers are
nearly all natives ; in fact, of the 268 teachers in the
schools of the Society in 1905, only eight were Europeans.
They are generally young men who have embraced
Christianity ; and Mr. Sargant, in his report, describes
them as often being men of real faith, and refers to their
earnestness and power of initiative.   But they are too few
in number, and as a rule they have received no adequate
training.   About 10 per cent. of them hold the third-class
teachers' certificate of Cape Colony : others have merely
passed Standards III. or IV. in the Basutoland schools.
The highest salaries are about £34 a year, but the chiefs
allow them land, and they often have common grazing
rights.   The missionaries generally interfere but little in
the working of the schools, and thus place great responsibility on the head teachers.   Some teachers aim at
becoming ministers, and, as the teaching profession is
regarded by the Basuto as an honourable one, a certain
prestige attaches to their position.   Mr. Sargant, however,
thought that they had insufficient opportunities of develop-
ing a real *esprit de corps*, and urged that the Government
should do more to recognise their work.

The standards adopted in these schools are those of the
Education Department of Cape Colony, but the curriculum
has been varied in one important particular—the native
language is used as the medium of instruction in the lower
standards, instead of English, as in the Cape schools.
Nevertheless, even in Basutoland the native language is
not taught satisfactorily, and the parents are sometimes
so eager that their children should learn English that they

refuse to pay for Sesuto school-books. Another weakness
in these schools is the general neglect of industrial training,
and the importance of this side of native education hardly
seems to have been sufficiently appreciated by the
missionaries of the Society. Hitherto the Society has had
great difficulty in collecting fees in its day-schools, and
it appears only to have been receiving about £300 a year
from this source. Recently, however, it has been endeavouring to enforce the payment of fees more systema-
tically.

The educational work of the Society has not been
confined to its schools. Its missionaries have prepared
Sesuto translations of the Bible—the work chiefly of
MM. Casalis and Mabille—and of the "Pilgrim's
Progress." They have also produced a Sesuto hymn-book
and a number of religious and educational works, and a
Sesuto paper, the *Leselinyana*, is issued every fortnight
from the Morija press.

The special position of the Paris Society naturally throws
the operations of other organisations somewhat into the
background. Nevertheless, excellent educational work
has been done both by the Roman Catholic and the
Church of England missions. The first Roman Catholic
mission was established at Roma in 1864, and since that
time it has opened several new stations and established a
number of schools. In 1905 this mission had ten registered
schools, including two boarding-schools for boys and girls
respectively at Roma; and according to the census of
1904 it then had 723 pupils. There are a few pupils at
the Roma schools in or above Standard IV., but practically
all the schools of the mission are for elementary education
only. The girls, who constitute the majority of the pupils
at Roma, are taught spinning, knitting, sewing, and house-
work. Unlike the Protestant missionaries, the Roman
Catholics very seldom employ native teachers, and in their

day-schools the instruction is given by unpaid sisters of the Holy Family of Bordeaux ; but the scarcity of European teachers has made it difficult for the mission to provide education even for the children of its own converts.

The English Church Mission established its first permanent station at Hlotse in 1876. It has subsequently opened other stations and has done much educational work. In 1905 it had 28 registered schools, and at the date of the census of 1904 it had 1,226 scholars. The chief educational institutions of this mission are its small normal and preparatory schools at Hlotse and Masite, at which manual training is given ; and a girls' school at Maseru, where some of the girls are taught laundry work. All the other Church of England schools seem to be elementary day-schools, similar in character to the day-schools of the Paris Society, native teachers being employed and small fees, amounting to a few shillings a year, being charged when practicable.

A few schools have been established by the natives themselves. One of these has been carried on by the native chief Joel, but apparently he soon lost interest in it, and its condition has not been satisfactory. Several schools, containing about 500 scholars, have during the last few years been opened by the African Methodist Episcopal Church, but hitherto Ethiopianism has made little headway in the country.

Valuable support has been given to the educational work by the Imperial Government, and previously by the Government of Cape Colony. After the annexation of Basutoland in 1871 the Cape Government made grants-in-aid to the Paris Society, and similar assistance was subsequently given to the Roman Catholic and Anglican missions. The Cape Government also established a model denominational school at Maseru, which was burnt during the Gun War in an attack on the town.   When the Imperial Government took over the country in 1884 the system of grants-in-aid was continued, and the Resident Commissioners have always been warm supporters of the educational work. The Cape Education Department, under Sir Langham Dale and Dr. Muir, has also continued to show a practical interest in the education of Basuto students, and from time to time has given much valuable help and advice.   No separate Education Department for Basutoland has yet been established, but an Education Officer was provisionally appointed in 1906–7. Previously the aided schools had been inspected annually by two District Commissioners or their assistants, and occasionally by a trained inspector, reports of the inspections being sent to the Resident Commissioner.

During recent years there has been a substantial increase in the amount of the Government grants. In 1897–8 the expenditure of the Government on education was £3,746 ; in 1906–7 it had risen to £14,000 (including the expenditure on the industrial school at Maseru).   It must, however, be remembered that between these dates the hut-tax had been raised from 10s. to £1, and that, as an inducement to the Basuto to acquiesce in the change, Lord Milner assured them that the Government would spend further sums in assisting education. The French missionaries appear to have hoped that the increase in the grant would have been on a still more liberal scale, and it is not very clear that it has fully satisfied the Basuto themselves.

In 1898 the late paramount chief, Lerothodi, handed over to the Government a sum of money which he had collected from his people for the purpose of establishing a central industrial institution. Owing to the late war, the execution of this scheme had to be postponed, but in 1904 the Government again took the matter up. A site near Maseru was selected by the Resident Commissioner, and, in addition to the sum contributed by the Basuto, amounting to £4,559, Lord Milner authorised a Government expenditure of £5,000, during the three years 1905–8, on the necessary buildings and equipment. By January 1906 a portion of the building had been completed, and the school was opened under Mr. Fogarty as director. A few weeks later Lord Selborne laid the foundation-stone of the main school building, which has since been completed. The institution comprises departments for builders, blacksmiths, carpenters, waggon-makers, and engineers, and provides accommodation for eighty pupils. The Basuto have been eager to take advantage of the training it offers, seventy applications for admission having been received before the school was opened, and much useful work has already been done by the pupils in the various departments.

The Government has also for some time past given assistance to successful scholars to enable them to obtain secondary education and industrial training at Lovedale or at other similar institutions in Cape Colony or Natal. Some of the leading Basuto chiefs have received their education at the Zonnebloem College, which, in accordance with the intention of its founders, is still frequented, though in a less degree than formerly, by the sons and relatives of chiefs.

It is stated that the high wages earned by educated natives during the late war gave a considerable stimulus to the educational movement in Basutoland. At any rate there seems to be no doubt that the desire for instruction is growing. Children often walk long distances to school. Parents are taking more interest in education, especially in districts under the charge of native ministers. Labour, materials, and money for building schools are freely supplied, and the rich congregations help the poorer to raise the necessary funds. Although it has been difficult to collect fees in the day-schools, Mr. Sargant estimated in 1906 that the total contributions from natives in Basutoland towards the cost of education were about equal to the mission funds derived from foreign sources. How considerable the growth of the educational work has been during the last few years may be gathered from a comparison of the statistics for 1898–9 with those for 1906–7. In the former year there. were 169 schools on the Government books, with 10,348 scholars; in 1906–7 the number of these schools had risen to 250, with 12,275 scholars.

Mr. Sargant's report to the Resident Commissioner in 1906 contains a number of valuable recommendations for the improvement of the educational system, which may be briefly summarised as follows :

Efficient and economical as the administration of the Paris Society undoubtedly is, the work of the Society has outgrown its organisation ; and the time has now come for more intimate co-operation by the Government and for the establishment of an Education Department with a staff of inspectors. The Government should arrange for the opening of schools in those parts of the country where none exist and where no mission is willing to provide them, and should increase its grants to the missionary societies. A central advisory board should be constituted, consisting of the Government Secretary as chairman, the Director of Education as vice-chairman, and five members appointed by the Resident Commissioner, of whom three would be representatives of the Paris Evangelical Mission Society, one of the English Church, and one of the Roman Catholics. One of the Paris Evangelical Society's representatives should be a native, and a separate representative of the natives should ultimately be added. Training should be given in all elementary schools in " manual occupations leading up to familiar native industries " (*e.g.* straw-plaiting, moulding of clay, bead- and wire-work), and for girls in sewing and knitting. In schools of a higher class instruction might be given in native industries, drawing, elementary physical measurements and observations, carpentry and gardening; and girls could be taught sewing, knitting, washing, ironing, dressmaking, cooking, and other domestic work. In special institutions gardening, elementary agriculture and forestry should also be taught. The teaching of European trades should be confined to a few specially equipped institutions. In the most elementary village schools arithmetic and the reading and writing of Sesuto should constitute the chief subjects of instruction, and English should only be taught, if at all, as a spoken language. The course should not be of more than three years, and every Mosuto child should pass through such a school and should there learn something of the handicrafts of his country. The next higher type of elementary school should be arranged in two divisions, the lower division being similar to the ordinary village school, and the upper division receiving instruction in English and inexpensive European industries; and in both divisions arithmetic should be adopted as the basis of classification. The most advanced type should have three divisions. Thus the Government, in Mr. Sargant's opinion, should recognise three grades of elementary schools, the lowest giving instruction in sub-standards, with no reading or writing of English; the next giving instruction up to Standard III.; and the highest up to Standard VI. Proper arrangements should be made for inspection and examinations; and vacation courses should be held for the teachers.

These important and far-reaching recommendations were submitted to the Resident Commissioner by Mr. Sargant after conferring with representatives of the various missions and they will no doubt carry great weight. They obviously involve a considerable increase in expenditure, but, as the Government has a substantial balance in hand representing accumulated surplus of revenue over expenditure, the financial side of the question does not seem to present insuperable difficulties, and the results of education in Basutoland may well encourage the Government to incur some further responsibility.   The Basuto are no longer the turbulent people whom the strong hand of Moshesh could hardly control.   Although they still retain their arms, they have become a loyal, and on the whole an orderly and peaceable community.   The most independent native people in South Africa, they are also probably the most prosperous and industrious.   Education has given them new wants and new incentives to labour ; and every year many thousands of them seek temporary employment outside Basutoland, and thus provide a valuable supply of labour for the neighbouring colonies.[1]   This remarkable change in the national character cannot of course be attributed solely to education.   In part it is due to the ability and wisdom of the paramount chiefs ; in part also to the admirable system of administration introduced by Sir Marshal Clarke and to the firmness and tact of the Resident Commissioners.   But the spirit of progress which is steadily permeating the country had its birth in the unpretentious schools of the missionaries.

§ 5. THE TRANSVAAL

Educational work among the Transvaal natives was initiated by the Hermannsburg Evangelical Lutheran and the Berlin Missionary Societies, who established their first missions in 1857 and 1860 respectively.   After many years they were followed by the Dutch Reformed Church, the

[1] In 1906–7, which was a good year, with plentiful rains, 76,785 labour passes were issued to Basuto seeking employment in various parts of South Africa. In the previous year, which appears to have been a bad one, the number of these passes was 95,009.

Swiss Mission, the Wesleyans, the Church of England, and other religious bodies, including the African Methodist Episcopalian Church. By these societies and churches a number of schools for natives were established. The missionaries carried on their work under great difficulties, and they received no assistance from the Boer Government, beyond the occasional exemption of native teachers from the poll-tax. Consequently, the schools remained in a very primitive, inefficient condition, and education has made comparatively little progress among the natives.

After the late war the Executive Council collected statistics with regard to the schools established by the various organisations, and adopted a scheme, which came into operation at the beginning of 1904, for granting financial aid to such schools as complied with the official regulations. In 1904–5 there were in existence 276 schools for native children, with an enrolment of 17,912 pupils and 425 teachers. By the end of that year 172 of these schools (for the most part under the Dutch Reformed Church and the Berlin Mission) were registered under the scheme of the Executive Council, and were therefore in a position to receive grants-in-aid. At the close of 1906–7 the number of registered schools was 199; and during that year there was a total average enrolment in aided schools of 11,730 scholars and 339 teachers. The unaided schools in 1905–6 numbered 177, with 208 teachers and 8,492 pupils on the roll. Ten schools[1] have been opened for "coloured" children, and in 1906–7 the Government expenditure in respect of these schools was £4,931. The total average enrolment in these schools during that year was 668·7 boys and 586·4 girls. The native education grants for 1906–7 amounted to £7,941, including £1,949

[1] Some, if not all, of these appear to be Government schools. Under the Education Act of 1907 the Government can establish schools for native or "coloured" children, and institutions for native or "coloured" teachers,

for training teachers. The Education Department has declined to make grants to any school which is not under the supervision of a white missionary; and this rule, if still in force, might well be reconsidered, as a number of schools have been established by the African Methodist Episcopalian Church and other native bodies, and there seems to be no sufficient reason for refusing them grants, if they comply with the standard of efficiency required by the Department.

In the aided schools instruction is given in English, reading, spelling, writing, arithmetic, physical exercises, singing, elementary drawing, and in sewing (for girls), and industrial work, such as gardening, mat-weaving and basket-making (for boys). Standard III. is the limit fixed in the Government scheme. Some difficulty has been caused by the number of native languages existing in the Colony; and the Education Department, although it does not other-wise interfere with the teaching of the native languages, has been obliged, for the sake of uniformity, to prescribe English as the language for examination purposes. The children usually pay fees varying from 6d. to 1s. per month, but in some schools as much as 2s. a month is charged.

The official reports and the evidence given before the Native Affairs Commission show that most of the native schools are in a state of deplorable inefficiency. They are generally held in church buildings ill-adapted for educational purposes. In many cases seats and desks have not been provided, " squatting room " for the children having been thought sufficient. The education given is often of an extremely rudimentary kind. In 114 schools inspected during 1904 no less than 85·5 per cent. of the children in attendance were in the sub-standards, and only 1·5 per cent. had passed or reached Standard III. In 1905–6 only 65 out of the 305 native teachers held certificates; and the unsatisfactory condition of these schools is largely due to the inefficiency of the teaching staffs. Many teachers are incapable of giving instruction beyond Standard I., and comparatively few are competent to bring their pupils up to Standard III. Even of such ill-qualified teachers there is no adequate supply; but this no doubt is due in part to the low remuneration offered them, missionary superintendents often objecting to pay higher salaries than £18 to £24 a year—a rate of remuneration considerably lower than that of a labourer in the mines. Absence of adequate provision for the training of teachers is a fatal defect in the present educational system. The only training institutions recognised by the Government seem to be the Wesleyan school at Kilnerton, a Swiss Mission school, the new training school opened at Bothsabelo by the Berlin Mission, and another near Pietersburg established in 1906 by the Church of England. In 1906-7 these four schools provided instruction for 117 students. In the absence of adequate training schools, the Education Department has held or supervised short instruction courses for teachers, which have been greatly appreciated.

Industrial instruction is given at the Endhlozana, Kilnerton, and Shiluvane institutions, and at some schools in the Zoutpansberg, but hitherto neither the missionary superintendents nor the natives have shown much enthusiasm for this expensive but important side of educational work. The provision of industrial schools was contemplated in the educational scheme prepared by the Government, and it may be hoped that something will shortly be done in this direction.

There seems to be no provision to meet the needs of natives who wish to give their children higher education, unless the children are trained as pupil teachers. Natives who desire such education for their children but do not intend that they should become teachers, have therefore to send them to institutions outside the Colony.

In 1906 the office of Superintendent of Native Education was abolished, and the native schools were placed under the district inspectors.[1]   It was hoped that this change would at any rate make it possible to carry out annual inspections of all the aided schools.   In this and other ways the Education Department has been endeavouring to improve the condition of the native schools, but the lack of funds has been a fatal obstacle to rapid progress.   Large as are the amounts collected from the natives in taxes, the sums voted for native education have hitherto been wholly inadequate ; and the opposition to any attempt to increase these contributions indicates that the importance of native education as a factor in the prosperity of the Colony is as yet very imperfectly recognised.   Nevertheless, the educational system has now at least been placed on a more satisfactory basis, and the recognition of the native schools by the Government has opened the door to new possibilities of further progress.   The traditions of the Colony are opposed to any rapid advance in this direction, but native educationists will doubtless in time establish their claim to more sympathetic consideration. At present the urgent needs are for more adequate grants-in-aid, the establishment and support of institutions for higher education, especially for teachers, and the provision of facilities for industrial training.

§ 6. THE ORANGE RIVER COLONY

Since about 1835 a number of missionary societies, of whom the Berlin and Wesleyan Societies were the pioneers, have been carrying on schools in this colony.   In 1878 the Government recognised the value of educational work by making a grant of £45 to the schools established

---

[1] The Zoutpansberg schools have been placed under a sub-inspector.

by the Dutch Reformed Church at Witzies Hoek ; and the
tribe of Paulus Mopeli consented to pay a special tax of
3s. 6d.[1] from each hut-owner towards the support of these
schools, the tax being collected for the mission by the
commandant.   In 1889 the Volksraad also made grants of
£30 and £50 respectively to the Berlin Society's schools at
Bethany and the Wesleyan school at Thaba' Nchu ; and
these schools, with the schools at Witzies Hoek, were placed
under the supervision of the Education Department. Since
the late war the Government has shown more active
interest in the subject.   It has established an industrial
school for girls at Thaba' Nchu, where plain cooking,
sewing, and laundry work are taught, and it has made
lump grants to various churches in proportion to the
number of pupils in the schools which they are respectively carrying on.   The total grants distributed in this
way during the year ending June 30, 1907, amounted
to £1,700.   Over a hundred schools were thus assisted
during the year, with an average attendance of 8,933
children. The natives themselves are fast awakening to
the advantages of education.   In July 1906 Mr. Hugh
Gunn, the Director of Education, informed the Legislative Council that the natives were determined to have
education whether the Government provided it or not ;
and that they willingly paid more in school fees than
the whites.   Their eagerness for education, he stated,
was pathetic.[2]

§ 7. Rhodesia

In 1860 the London Missionary Society opened a
station at Imyati, and it is now carrying on several schools

---

[1] The amount is now 10s.   A tax of a similar kind is in force at
Thaba' Nchu. See Report of the Director of Education for 1906-7,
p. 24.

[2] Reuter's report in the *Daily News*, of July 21, 1906.

for natives, including an industrial training institution at
Hopefountain. Little educational work was attempted
among the natives by other agencies until the Jesuits,
between 1890 and 1894, established a mission station at
Chishawasha, which has now become an important
educational institution, at which special attention is given
to gardening and agriculture, and instruction in various
trades. Subsequently the Jesuits opened a large
day-school at Empandeni, at which, as at Chishawasha,
prominence is given to industrial training. A flourish-
ing industrial institution was also established about
fifteen years ago by the American Board of Colonial
and Foreign Missions at Mount Silinda, on a site
selected by Mr. Rhodes, which is still the headquarters
of that mission. At this institution, which comprises
boarding- and day-schools, a sawmill and industrial
plant of considerable value have been set up, and good
technical instruction of various kinds is given, including
horticulture. The same society has a day-school at
Chikore, at which successful manual training is provided.
During recent years educational work has also been
carried on by the Church of England and by the Wesleyan,
Dutch Reformed and American Methodist Churches. At
the S. Augustine's native college (Church of England), at
Penhalonga, much time is devoted to farming, gardening,
brick-making, and building.

The Government has supported the missions by making
them grants of land, and since 1899 it has given some
financial assistance. But until 1907 the mission schools
could obtain grants-in-aid only on complying with
stringent conditions as to industrial training, the teaching of English, and the attendance of scholars. Instruction
in farming, gardening, and building, or other work has been
given in some of the better class schools, but the cost of
teaching trades, except at a few special institutions, is

extremely difficult.   Missionaries also have not always
found it easy to secure native teachers able to give the
required instruction in English, especially in districts
where little English is spoken.   Only three schools were
successful in 1906 in obtaining grants-in-aid.   In the
following year the Government issued new regulations
framed so as to enable a larger number of schools to share
in the grants.   Under these regulations thirty schools became entitled during the year to receive assistance from
the Government ; and it was anticipated that the number
of aided schools would be increased to forty-three in 1908.
The total amount of the Government grants during 1907
was £787.   In addition, a sum of £50 was contributed
to a coloured school at Bulawayo.   The Government has
sought to encourage the training of native girls in domestic
work, and in three schools are provided facilities for such
training.

The increased attention on the part of the Government
to native education will no doubt make the schools more
efficient, and it is to be hoped that in the future grants-in-
aid may be made on a more liberal scale.   Dr. Duthie, the
Director of Native Education, informed the Native Affairs
Commission four years ago that the Government hoped, as
revenue improved, to establish a better educational system.
By the changes effected in 1907 an important step has now
been taken towards the fulfilment of this hope.   Much still
remains to be done.   The foundations of a more satisfactory system have, however, been laid.

The natives are already beginning to show a keen
appreciation of the schools.   " Amongst the younger
generation," writes the Rev. E. H. Etheridge, the principal
of the S. Augustine's native college, " there is a great
desire for education.   Every vacancy for the next year is
already filled here.   We could easily double our numbers
if we had the means and accommodation."   He states

that scholars at S. Augustine's pay an entrance fee of £3 on entering the school, and that the college is largely maintained by their manual work on the farm. " I do not think," he says, " that at present (owing to increased taxation) they could contribute more." In some of the other schools the pupils pay fees varying from 6d. to 2s. a month.

Among the natives of Rhodesia are visible the same signs of progress as are seen in other parts of South Africa. Mr. Taylor, the Chief Native Commissioner for Matabeleland, in his report for 1903–4, draws attention to this forward tendency and the increasing need of education :

Owing to the rapid march of civilisation in this Protectorate (he writes) the development of the country by means of railways, and the establishment of a fully organised Administration, the progress of the natives has been more marked than in any other part of South Africa.

This is exemplified on every hand, but notably in ready compliance with legislation, in the growth already of the habit of work, in the extension and improvement of agricultural operations, and in the growing appreciation of the value of money.

Much, however, requires to be done in the direction of education, which infuses self-respect and discipline of mind and body, while dissipating ignorance. Good work is being done under this head by many of the missions, especially by those which recognise in industrial training a civilising agent of the highest value. As I pointed out last year, it is indispensable. In this connection I would make special mention of the excellent churches and schools, built entirely by local natives under skilled European guidance at the London Missionary Society's stations of Hopefountain and Dombadema ; and also of the efforts to improve agricultural methods which is a speciality of the Church of England's Mission on the Bembesi River. I am convinced that it is in this direction—i.e. in the sphere of stock-farming and agriculture, the natural occupation of the natives—that early efforts to elevate them should be made ; for so development will lead on to a gradual assimilation of civilisation in other phases, a sounder method than rude attempts to graft uncongenial occupations suddenly upon their lives. Time and patient effort may be trusted to broaden the natives' field of vision whilst improvement is sought upon their own ground first.

§ 8. THE BECHUANALAND PROTECTORATE

The London Missionary Society has established schools at five of the principal towns and in some outlying districts. At Serowe, the new town to which Khama has moved his people, the Society has a school with an enrolment of about 140 pupils, but none of the classes are above Standard III. There is a similar school at Kanye in Bathoen's country, and a poll-tax of 1s. a year is levied by the chief himself for educational purposes. Schools have also been carried on by the Lutheran and Dutch Reformed Mission and by some Ethiopian bodies ; and a native minister has a school near Lake Ngami with about a hundred boys and girls. The Bechuanas who desire higher education have usually gone to Lovedale or Morija, the Kuruman school having been closed. But the London Missionary Society has recently opened an important institution, under the Rev. H. W. Willoughby, at Tiger's Kloof, near Vryburg, for training teachers and providing industrial instruction, which should prove of great value to Bechuana boys from the Protectorate.

The Government gives the London Missionary Society and the Dutch Reformed Church financial assistance for their schools ; and during 1906–7 £750 was granted for this purpose, including a contribution for the Vryburg institution. On the whole, the progress of education in the Protectorate has not been satisfactory, although there has been a con-

siderable demand for the Sechuana publications which the
London Missionary Society has issued, and a large number
of the natives are said to read easily and to make use of the
post-office to communicate with their friends. It may be
hoped that the opening of the Vryburg institution will
supply a useful stimulus; but the Bechuanas, as a rule,
do not seem to possess the robust qualities that make
for rapid progress.

§ 9. Summary

Considering the difficulties under which the educational
work has been carried on in the various colonies, the
missionaries have achieved remarkably successful results.
Nevertheless, it is evident that the instruction given
in many of the schools is ill-adapted to the needs
of native children. The education generally has been
too " bookish." Sufficient attention has not always been
given to the development of character. The training of
eye and hand has too often been neglected ; many of the
school-books are not well adapted to native children ; and
the premature use of English as the medium of instruction
has greatly increased the difficulty of getting the children
to grasp the new ideas presented to them, and has led to
much fruitless learning by rote. It was natural that the
missionaries, when faced by the difficult problem of educating native children, should generally have adopted the
educational methods with which they were familiar, without sufficiently considering whether a system designed for
the educational needs of white children was adapted to
the different requirements of the natives. It was, however, very difficult for them to do otherwise. Their
financial position made the assistance of the various
Governments indispensable, and, in order to obtain grants-
in-aid, it was necessary to comply with the regulations of

the Education Departments, which have prescribed practically the same courses for native children as for white. This is now recognised to have been a serious error ; but at the present stage it is not easy to rectify it, for the natives, with their keen ambition to imitate the white man, set great value on a European education and would resent any attempt to deprive them of it. Still, it has become clear that, unless some change is made, native education will continue to produce defective and inadequate results ; and there has been great need that the question should be thoroughly investigated with a view to placing the educational systems of the various colonies on a more effective and uniform basis. An important step in this direction was taken by the South African Native Affairs Commission of 1903–5. The Commissioners obtained evidence from leading missionaries engaged in educational work, from officials of the Education Departments in the various colonies, and from a number of magistrates and others, including natives, representing many shades of opinion on educational matters ; they inspected Lovedale and other important institutions ; and, as the result of their inquiries, they came to the following conclusions :

" that education has been beneficial to the natives of South Africa and that its effect upon them has been to increase their capacity for usefulness and their earning power ; "

that compulsory education for natives is not advisable, and that no system of general public undenominational education, independent of existing missionary organisations, should be undertaken at present ;

that there is " need generally for more liberal total grants-in-aid of native education " ; and a majority of the Commissioners were of opinion that the same general support that is given to elementary education should be extended to some form of industrial training, and that recognition and aid should be given to native schools not under European control, if they comply with the official regulations ;

that local contributions are more satisfactorily collected in the form of a rate for educational purposes than by the payment of school fees or the collection of voluntary subscriptions by headmen ;

"that any local demand for native education not otherwise provided for should be met by the creation of a fund to be administered or not, as circumstances permit, by a local board or committee, and to be raised by means of a rate levied upon the natives in the area concerned, such rate to count in lieu of school fees to those who pay the rate" ; and that in such cases Government aid should be given.

And, as matters of immediate practical possibility, the Commissioners recommend :

"the continuance of Government grants-in-aid of native elementary education ; "

"that special encouragement and support by way of grants-in-aid be given to such schools and institutions as give efficient industrial training ; "

"that a central native college or similar institution be established, and aided by the various States, for training native teachers and in order to afford opportunities for higher education to native students ; "

"that it should be recognised as a principle that natives receiving educational advantages for themselves or their children should contribute towards the cost :—in the matter of elementary education and industrial training by payment of school fees or a local rate, and as to higher education by payment of adequate students' fees ; "

"that, where possible, in schools for natives there should be instruction in the elementary rules of hygiene ; "

"that, where it is possible, workshops and school farms

in connection with elementary native schools should
receive a special measure of encouragement and support ; "

" that the question of the curriculum for native schools
should be dealt with by a conference composed of educational experts and men of experience among the natives,"
and "that moral and religious instruction should be given in
all native schools"; that the native language should be used
as the medium of instruction in the lower standards, English
being treated as a separate study ; that the text-books and
reading lessons in the native language should " impress on
the minds of the pupils, among other useful matters, simple
scientific and sanitary principles, temperance, and the
elementary rules of hygiene."

In support of their recommendation that the education of
the natives should in the main be left to voluntary agencies
as in the past, the Commissioners point out that " there
would be a distinct loss in the separation of secular instruction from moral and religious influences," and that
" the cost of any general scheme for establishment of
undenominational schools for native children would be
prohibitive." But they acknowledge the need of some
further organisation in places where no voluntary school
has been provided, and of increased Government grants.

While emphasising the importance of manual and industrial training, the Commissioners recognise that advanced
technical instruction can only be given with advantage
at a few specially equipped institutions, and a minority
of them were of opinion that all technical instruction beyond simple manual training should be treated as a separate
course, apart from elementary education. The minority
are supported in this respect by Mr. Sargant, and, considering the difficulty and expense of teaching European
trades, it seems at least doubtful whether a combination of
the elementary school and the workshop is practicable or
desirable. Further assistance for technical education is

much needed, for instruction of this kind involves heavy expenditure, and missionary societies do not always appreciate its importance, and perhaps naturally regard it as somewhat outside the scope of their work. The manual training at the elementary schools, while an essential part of the course, might be of a comparatively simple character, designed to train the eye and hand and to develop habits of application, but limited to such matters as gardening and agriculture and familiar native industries (*e.g.* the making of baskets and water-pitchers, bead-work, and the stitching of skins, with sewing and knitting for girls).

The recommendation of the Commissioners that the native languages should be substituted for English as the medium of instruction in the lower standards, is of special value, for the practice of giving instruction in English is probably one of the chief reasons why so many of the children leave school without having acquired even the rudiments of useful knowledge. The failure of the natives in the higher educational standards has often been commented on ; it has perhaps not been sufficiently considered how far this failure has been due to the premature use of English, combined with defective teaching and unsuitable school-books in the elementary schools. And the native languages have a special educational value, which should not be overlooked. "They are splendidly built," writes the Rev. H. A. Junod, in a paper addressed to the Superintendents of Education in the Transvaal and the Orange River Colony "they possess a wonderful richness in grammatical forms and ways of expressing ideas. They are the best inheritance which their forefathers have left to the actual natives of these countries. When he speaks his vernacular, the Zulu, the Thonga, is a man. When he speaks a European language, he is too often a caricature. Why, therefore, is the study of those languages so much abandoned, if not entirely overlooked, in most of the South African schools ?

It is placed only in Standards I. to II. ; it seems that it must be put out of the way as soon as possible, to be replaced entirely by English. I quite agree that the natives must learn English, that the possession of it is a wonderful means of development ; but they are Bantu none the less, and ought not to despise their beautiful mother-tongue. I think they ought to be thoroughly instructed in its grammatical structure. It is the best way for them to accustom themselves to grasp abstract ideas, in remaining on their own ground ; and my experience has shown me that there is no better intellectual exercise than parsing a sentence of their own tongue in a terminology which must try to be as genuine as possible." Not only with regard to the use of the native languages, but in reference to other matters as well, it is to be hoped that curricula will be devised to meet the special needs of native children. In many ways it may be advisable to differentiate between the education given in the native and in the white schools. The children of tribal natives need special training in view of their superstitions, the conditions of their home-life, and the change to unfamiliar surroundings for which they have to be prepared. Native children also have special aptitudes and qualities, which ought to be carefully developed. In the case of the detribalised natives any substantial variation from the ordinary European curriculum may be difficult in view of their desire to have the same education as the whites ; but, at any rate for tribal natives, it may be well to introduce a somewhat different system, and special care should be taken to cultivate characteristic tribal gifts and virtues, such as eloquence, imagination, fortitude, and obedience to law.

The Commissioners' recognition of the need of State aid for the provision of higher education for natives at a central college is a notable fact in the progress of native education. Hitherto the Colonial Governments have

refused to assist higher education, except for the purpose
of training native teachers, and the Commissioners'
proposal, if carried out effectively, will remove a real
grievance, for at present the natives who desire and are
willing to pay for higher education have considerable
reason for dissatisfaction. The scheme was warmly
supported by the late Dr. Stewart of Lovedale, and great
efforts have been made to ensure its fulfilment. An
executive committee was formed by the leading natives in
King William's Town, with Mr. J. W. Weir as chairman ;
meetings in support of the project were held by the
natives in the various colonies ; and in December 1905, a
few days after the death of Dr. Stewart, a representative
convention, attended by about a hundred and sixty
delegates from Cape Colony, Basutoland, and the Transvaal, met at Lovedale to concert measures to bring the
matter before the various Governments in a practical
form. At this meeting a petition to the High Commissioner and the Governors of Cape Colony and Natal
in support of the proposed college was approved ; arrangements were made for obtaining signatures and for raising
a guarantee fund ; and a committee was appointed to
submit to the various Governments a scheme for acquiring
a suitable site for the new college. The movement has
now made such progress that its success seems to be
assured. The interest and enthusiasm of the natives have
" surprised even those who know them best." [1] Meetings
have been held in many parts of South Africa approving
the scheme, and by February 1907 a fund of between
£40,000 and £50,000 had been raised or promised by the
natives and their European supporters, including a contribution of £10,000 voted by the Transkeian General
Council. Churches and missionary societies, laying aside
sectarian differences, have expressed their readiness to

[1] *The Christian Express* of December 1, 1906, p. 274.

co-operate in the working of the college ; and the Cape
Government has approached the other Colonial Governments, through the High Commissioner, to secure their
co-operation in contributing to its support. It is understood that these Governments have expressed their
willingness to assist, and that a commission will probably
be appointed, representing the contributing Governments
and the native subscribers, to report as to the practical
steps to be taken for the establishment and working of
the new institution. Great care will no doubt be needed
in working out the details of the scheme ; and it has yet
to be seen whether a sufficient number of students capable
of taking advantage of an institution of this character
will be forthcoming. A site near Lovedale has now been
selected for the new college, subject to the approval of the
various Governments; and it is difficult to see how a better
choice could be made. Lovedale has long been the chief
centre of the native educational movement, and without the
unique influence of Dr. Stewart and the practical demon-
stration which he supplied in the Lovedale classes that his
educational ideals were based on a sound estimate of the
capabilities of the natives, the establishment of any
adequate institution for their higher education might well
have proved impracticable.

Enough has been said to show how important a factor
the native school has become in the social and economic
development of South Africa. It is estimated that at the
present time over 150,000 native and coloured children
are receiving education, and this number will doubtless
increase rapidly as the desire for education spreads among
the tribal natives. The embittered controversies which
marked the early days of the missionary movement are
now gradually passing into oblivion; the Governments of
all the colonies are giving the mission schools increasing
assistance ; and the officials of the Education Departments

and many of the magistrates take a keen interest in their
progress. Nevertheless, racial prejudices have hitherto
been strong enough to prevent even the most progressive
of the Colonial Governments from adopting as energetic
a policy as the importance of the question demands.
This is greatly to be regretted, for an efficient system of
native education is essential to the development of South
Africa. It is necessary, in the first place, for the protection of the natives, who are now drawn in increasing
numbers to the towns and other centres of industry.
These natives are accustomed to live under the authority
of their chiefs and the restraints and moral standards
which tribal custom enforces. They are now removed
from these influences and brought suddenly into contact
with the unfamiliar freedom of civilised life. This
contact exposes them to temptations which they are ill
prepared to resist, and it is hardly surprising that the
reports of the magistrates too often tell a deplorable tale
of the demoralisation of fine tribal natives in the towns.
Against these dangers there has been no more effective
protection for the native than the education and religious
training provided in a good mission school; and this
training may well be regarded as an indispensable
stage in the transformation of tribal natives into wage-
earners at industrial centres. Again, education is necessary
to enable natives to render the services which are needed
from them both by the whites and by their own people,
and by so doing to improve their own position. A native
who has a knowledge of English, who can read and write,
and has received some manual training, is incomparably
more useful than the rude tribal Kafir even as an ordinary
labourer. It is sometimes said that education unfits the
natives for manual work. This statement is misleading.
Natives who have made satisfactory progress in the schools
no doubt often try to turn their education to account by

obtaining more remunerative employment than that of a
manual labourer. But most native scholars acquire only
an extremely elementary education, and, although some of
them get exaggerated ideas of their accomplishments and
affect to despise manual work, very many make excellent
labourers. Moreover, as Sir Henry Elliot pointed out
before the Native Affairs Commission, when education
becomes more general the ordinary educated native will
have less temptation to regard himself as on a higher level
than his fellows. And it must be remembered that natives
are needed for many kinds of work for which education is
essential. Many of them are employed by the whites
as messengers, policemen, artisans, hospital assistants,
clerks, teachers, interpreters, and in similar occupations ;
and amongst their own people there is an increasing need
of native doctors, nurses, and artisans. The employment
of whites in these capacities would often be impracticable
in view of the high wages which they require, and it is
desirable that a sufficient number of properly qualified
natives should be forthcoming. Education also is an important factor in providing motives for industry. Frequent
complaints are made of the difficulty of obtaining an
adequate supply of native labour. It is often said that
the native is indolent and must be taught the "dignity of
labour." Gradually, however, it is being recognised that
the true cause of the difficulty is to be found, not in any
inherent defect in the character of the natives, but in the
absence of a sufficient motive to engage in continuous
work. Uneducated natives can satisfy their primitive
needs with little exertion ; and if they are content with
their present earnings, the difficulty of obtaining labour is
not likely to disappear. But the progress of education
tends inevitably to raise the standard of living, and by
creating fresh needs supplies a powerful incentive to
labour. And from the point of view of the white

colonists there are other reasons of still greater weight
for educating the natives. Nothing could be more un-
worthy, or in the long run more disastrous, than that the
whites in South Africa should regard the natives as a
mere "labour asset." If this view prevailed—and it is to
be feared that it still has some advocates—it would
inevitably result in the demoralisation of the white
communities. "We have to bear in mind," writes Sir
Marshal Clarke, "that where two races on different planes
of civilisation come into such close contact as do the
whites and blacks in South Africa, they act and react on
each other, and where the higher race neglects its duty to
the lower it will itself suffer."[1] Neglect of this duty has
many serious consequences, but perhaps none more
disastrous than its effects on the white children.
Mr. P. A. Barnett, the late Director of Education in
Natal, in his report for 1904, draws special attention to
this vital matter. "Of the baser and more cruel contamination," he says, "liable to result from the intimate
domestic contact of little European children with people
whose life, thoughts, and speech are habitually at a low
level, it is hard to speak in the measured terms that
decorum requires. One may have the most real respect
for the Zulu folk in their places, and in regard to the stage
of their development: but, apart from the hard pressure
of social difficulty, here, where so many influences fight
against the refinement and elevation of life, little Zulu
drudges are the worst trainers of youth that we can
employ." As Mr. Barnett justly says, "the mental and
moral development of the white children is inextricably
involved in that of the black."

The South African colonists appear to be realising,
though somewhat tardily and slowly, the force of these

[1] Special Reports on Educational Subjects, vol. xiii. part II. (Cd.
2378), Appendix B 4.

considerations, and the recent developments of the
education movement suggest that a change of public
opinion on the subject is gradually taking place. The
last few years have in fact been a time of remarkable
advance in many directions. The desire for education
has been spreading more widely among the natives.
They have been active in promoting the establishment
of new institutions for higher education and industrial
training, and they have contributed freely to the funds
required for these purposes. They have also shown a
more self-reliant spirit than in the past and a new
capacity for organisation. The native churches have
already established a number of elementary day-schools,
and have been sending boys to negro colleges in America
for higher education. No doubt this new activity on
the part of the natives has in it a strong element of
racial feeling, but, if wisely directed, it contains much
promise for the future. And the forward movement
has not been confined to the natives. The value of
the educational work has received official recognition in
the report of the Native Affairs Commission, and the
recommendations of the Commissioners have provided a
basis for a more progressive educational policy. The
attitude which the Colonial Governments have recently
adopted indicates that they are beginning to realise the
importance of securing an efficient system of native
education. In the Transvaal native schools have for the
first time been recognised and assisted by the State. In
the Orange River Colony there has been a considerable
extension of the system of granting aid already in force.
And in both these colonies the Education Departments
have begun to take active steps to promote the efficiency
of the schools. In the other colonies the grants-in-aid
have been increased, and a gradual improvement seems to
be taking place in the character of the schools. And,

lastly, by the decision of the Colonial Governments to co-operate in supporting the proposed native college, the need of providing facilities for higher education has at length been recognised.

NOTES

Mr. E. B. Sargant's Report on Native Education in South Africa.—Since the above chapter was written the third part of this report, dealing with education in the Protectorates, has been published[1]. It contains an extremely interesting analysis of the special problems of native education in Basutoland and the Bechuanaland Protectorate, and a number of valuable recommendations for placing the native schools on a more satisfactory basis. It will no doubt be carefully studied by those who are directly concerned in educational work, and there is much in it which claims the attention of a wider circle of readers.

The Lovedale Institution.—According to the report of this institution for 1907, the number of pupils on the roll in that year was as follows :

Boys' side—		
Native boarders, pupils	323	
,, ,, apprentices	115	
,, day-pupils	55	
Europeans	14	
		507
Girls' side—		
Native boarders, pupils	109	
,, ,, apprentices	55	
,, day-pupils	32	
Europeans	10	
		206
Elementary School	181	
Total		894

The pupils were divided as follows between the various departments of the institution :

[1] Colonial Reports, Miscellaneous, No. 52 (Cd. 4119).

| | NATIVES. | | | | EUROPEANS. | | TOTAL. |
| | Boarders. | | Day Pupils. | | | | |
	Boys.	Girls.	Boys.	Girls.	Boys.	Girls.	
College Department—							
Matriculation Class .	7	—	—	—	1	—	8
School Higher Class—							
Senior Division .	25	2	3	—	3	—	33
Junior Division .	23	—	4	—	3	—	30
							— 71
Normal Department—							
Third year . . .	16	6	—	—	—	—	22
Second year . . .	17	19	2	—	—	—	38
First year . . .	—	—	—	—	—	—	
Section A . .	34	—	1	—	—	—	35
Section B . .	35	—	1	—	—	—	36
Section C . .	—	22	—	—	—	—	22
							— 153
School Department—							
Boys, Standard VI. .	71	—	11	—	2	—	84
,, V. .	61	—	22	—	—	—	83
,, IV. .	34	—	11	—	1	—	46
Girls, Standard VI. .	—	25	—	9	—	1	35
,, V. .	—	17	—	14	—	—	31
,, IV. .	—	12	—	9	—	1	22
							— 301
Elementary School—							
Standard III. . .	15	1	7	15	—	—	38
,, II. . .	8	—	12	15	—	—	35
,, I. . .	3	—	9	7	—	—	19
Sub-standard B . .	—	—	11	24	—	—	35
,, A . .	—	—	21	33	—	—	54
							— 181
Separate Class—							
Standard II. . .	1	4	—	—	3	3	11
Sub-Standard . .	—	1	—	—	1	5	7
							— 18
Industrial Departments—							
Girls' work . .	—	51	—	—	—	—	51
Waggon-making .	11	—	—	—	—	—	11
Printing . .	14	—	—	—	—	—	14
Bookbinding .	3	—	—	—	—	—	3
Shoemaking .	4	—	—	—	—	—	4
Carpentry . .	38	—	—	—	—	—	38
Technical . .	29	—	—	—	—	—	29
Office . .	5	—	—	—	—	—	5
Book Store .	3	—	—	—	—	—	3
Hospital . .	5	4	—	—	—	—	9
Post Office . .	3	—	—	—	—	—	3
							— 170
Totals .	465	164	115	126	14	10	894

During the year 2 pupils (out of 4 presented) passed the Matriculation, 4 (out of 19 presented) passed the University School Higher Examination, and 67 (out of 146 presented) passed the Government Normal Examination, of whom 14 were in the third-year, 17 in the second-year, and 36 in the first-year classes respectively.

The fees paid by natives during the year amounted to £5,503 9s. 7d. The total sum so paid by natives since 1870 is no less than £83,988 3s. 10d.

CHAPTER VII

THE ETHIOPIAN MOVEMENT: NATIVE
CHURCHES [1]

ONE sign of the growth of a more independent, progressive spirit among the natives is the formation during recent years of a number of self-governing native churches. All or most of these churches owe their origin to secessions from European missions. Their racial character has caused no little anxiety among the white communities in South Africa. The effects of the movement are likely to be felt far beyond church affairs. It is worth while to examine its origin and progress, and to discover so far as possible the objects which the new native churches have in view.

The beginning of the movement may be traced to the formation, about the year 1886, of a small native church in Tembuland, known as "the Church of the Tembus," by

[1] Many of the particulars given in this chapter have been obtained from a paper on "The Ethiopian Movement," read by the Rev. F. B. Bridgman, at the Natal Missionary Conference in July 1903, and from a number of articles on Ethiopianism published in *The Christian Express* (Lovedale) during the years 1901–3. Much information with regard to various phases of the movement is contained in the evidence given before the South African Native Affairs Commission, 1903–5, by missionaries, leaders of native churches, and others. The account of the Order of Ethiopia is based mainly on two articles in *The East and the West* (January 1903 and October 1904) by the Rev. F.W. Puller, formerly chaplain to the Order, and the Rev. W. M. Cameron (the present Coadjutor-Bishop of Cape Town), also a former chaplain and now Acting Provincial of the Order, and on the Rev. J. M. Dwane's evidence before the Native Affairs Commission.

an ex-Wesleyan preacher named Nehemiah Tile. Tile's followers afterwards became Baptists, and are popularly known as Ethiopians. They are few in number, and the secession would be of little importance had it not suggested the idea of a much wider movement some four years later. Some Wesleyan natives at Johannesburg desired to undertake evangelical work. The Wesleyan authorities did not see their way to sanction this ; and the natives, under the leadership of the Rev. M. M. Makone, formed themselves into a separate body on Wesleyan lines. They called their new organisation " The Ethiopian Church," and this name has given the whole separatist movement its popular designation of " Ethiopianism." In 1894 they were joined by another secessionist from the Wesleyan Church, the Rev. J. M. Dwane, who speedily became one of their leading members. Mr. Dwane was a nephew of the chief of the Amantinde, a sub-tribe of the Gaikas. His father quarrelled with the chief and removed to another sub-tribe, the Amagqunukwebe, where he became a councillor of their chief, Kama, and his daughter married Kama's son or brother. Mr. Dwane was born after his father removed to the Amagqunukwebe, about the year 1848. As a boy he came under the influence of Mr. Lamplough, a Wesleyan missionary, and was educated at the Wesleyan institution at Healdtown. Here he was trained as a teacher, and for three years he acted as a schoolmaster. He then began work as a missionary, and in 1881 he was ordained. For about thirteen years he discharged his duties as a Wesleyan minister, and in 1894 he was in charge of a mission station at Mount Coke, near King William's Town. In that year he went to England, with the approval of his superiors, and collected money for an institution connected with his mission. On returning to South Africa he reported the results of his journey to the Wesleyan authorities at Cape Town. Difficulties then arose with

regard to the money which he had received. The Wesleyan authorities insisted that by the rules of their body
it should be paid into their general fund. Mr. Dwane
maintained that it should be applied for the purposes of
the institution for which it had been collected. He paid it,
as requested, into the general fund, but after this controversy
he left the Wesleyans and joined the Ethiopian Church
with a considerable number of followers. He soon dis-
covered that his new church lacked efficient organisation
and discipline ; and in 1896 he visited the United States
on a deputation to the African Methodist Episcopal
Church (generally known as the A.M.E. Church), in
the hope that these defects might be remedied by an
amalgamation with that body. After examining the work of
this negro church in various states and making arrangements
for the proposed union, he returned to South Africa as the
general superintendent of the A.M.E. Church in that
country, and at a large representative conference of the
Ethiopians held at Lesseyton in April 1897 he received
a number of the ministers and delegates present into the
A.M.E. Church. The work of affiliation proceeded rapidly,
and in 1898 Bishop Turner, the senior bishop of that
church, came to South Africa to inspect the work of the
Ethiopian Church and to complete arrangements for the
amalgamation. During the six or eight weeks which
he spent in the country he consecrated Mr. Dwane as
a vicar-bishop, confirmed his action at the Lesseyton
conference, organised annual conferences at Pretoria and
Queenstown, and ordained about sixty local preachers as
deacons and elders. On his return to America, his colleagues appear to have made some difficulty about ratifying
these acts ; and the question of the union was postponed
until their next quadrennial conference. In 1898 Mr. Dwane
again visited America, but he failed to obtain the official
recognition he desired. During this visit he became dis-

satisfied as to the validity of the orders in the A.M.E. Church, and with regard to the strained relations which he found existing, not only between whites and blacks, but also between the lighter and darker coloured members of that church.   These features of the A.M.E. Church, or, as his critics suggest, its delay in confirming his appointment by Bishop Turner, revived doubts which he had originally felt as to the wisdom of the proposed amalgamation.   On returning to South Africa he expressed his dissatisfaction to his fellow Ethiopians, advising them, if they wished an organisation of their own, to apply for assistance to " the people on the spot, who brought the Gospel to you."   In 1899, by the advice of the Rector of Queenstown, he sub-mitted to the Archbishop of Cape Town an application that the Ethiopian Church should be given a distinct organisation within the Anglican Church.   Before dealing with this application, the Archbishop desired to be satisfied that it was approved by the members of the Ethiopian Church.   Mr. Dwane accordingly arranged a conference of that body at Queenstown.   The war prevented represen-tatives from the Transvaal and Orange River Colony attending this meeting.   But all the ministers of the Ethiopian Church in Cape Colony appear to have been present, and the following resolutions were passed with only four dissentients, who at once left the conference :

1. That, having regard to the great importance of Christian unity, and being convinced that the scriptural and historical safeguard of the same is the Catholic Episcopate, this conference resolves to petition his Grace the Archbishop of Cape Town and the other Bishops of the Church of the Province of South Africa to give our body a valid Episcopate and Priesthood, and to make such arrangements as may be found possible to include our body within the fold of the Catholic Church on the lines indicated in our Superin-tendent's letter to the Bishop of Cape Town.
2. That this conference accepts and embraces the

Doctrine, Sacraments, and Discipline of Christ, as the same are contained in Holy Scripture, according as the Church of England has set forth the same in its Standards of Faith and Doctrine.

These resolutions were communicated to the Archbishop of Cape Town, who instituted careful inquiries as to the character of the Ethiopian body. In 1900 a synod was held at Grahamstown, at which the Archbishop and the Bishops of the province met Mr. Dwane and the other Ethiopian representatives to discuss the application made by the Queenstown conference. The result was an agreement that an Order, to be called " The Order of Ethiopia," should be formed within the Church of England, with a Provincial and Chapter, and with the Archbishop as Visitor. The Chapter was to have power, with episcopal approval, to frame a constitution and rules. The property of the Order was to be vested in trustees upon trusts to be sanctioned by the Visitor after consultation with the Provincial. Each member was to become a member of the Anglican Church before admission to the Order. Suitable ex-ministers were to be licensed as readers, catechists, and sub-deacons ; and arrangements were to be made for preparing candidates for orders. If at any time a bishop should be appointed over the Order, he was to exercise episcopal functions under, and at the request of, the bishop of the diocese. The Order was to be under the jurisdiction of the bishop, but not of the parochial clergy. Since 1899 Mr. Dwane and the other Ethiopian ministers had been conducting services with the sanction of the Anglican bishops, but had ceased to administer the sacraments. Mr. Dwane was now admitted into the Church of England, and was confirmed and appointed Provincial of the Order, and four months later he was ordained as a deacon. Three other members of the Order have subsequently been admitted to the diaconate, and about twelve have received catechists' licences after careful preparation under white chaplains. More than fourteen hundred natives connected with the Order have been confirmed, and Mr. Dwane estimated that in 1903 there were about five thousand members of the Order in Cape Colony.

The great majority of the Ethiopians who took part in the conference at Queenstown joined the Order, but the dissentient minority refused to accept the decision of that conference, and remained affiliated to the A.M.E. Church. Owing to the late war Mr. Dwane was unable to communicate with the members of the Ethiopian Church in the Transvaal and the Orange River Colony while the negotiations with the Archbishop of Cape Town were in progress, and after the war the Order was not able to carry on work in these colonies. Most of these Ethiopians have therefore probably remained members of the A.M.E. Church. The Order appears to have no representatives in Natal.

The Order has hitherto been in somewhat troubled waters. There has been considerable friction with the A.M.E. Church, and a chapel at Debe has been successfully claimed by the minority of the congregation, who refused to follow Mr. Dwane. There has also been trouble with a hostile faction in the Amagqunukwebe tribe ; and Dr. Cameron, the Coadjutor-Bishop of Cape Town, who for some time acted as chaplain to the Order, stated that on several occasions his students were reduced to the verge of starvation. The work of the Order has been further hampered by want of money and by the inadequate education of its local preachers. Many of these preachers, however, seem anxious to obtain the training needed to fit them for their work. Dr. Cameron stated in 1904 that "what they lacked in knowledge they made up, with few exceptions, in application, shrewdness, and keenness to learn"; and the present chaplain, the Rev. W. A. Goodwin, reports : " I found my students very keen Churchmen, exceedingly reverent, ready evangelists, and astonishingly careless of money advantages. They reminded me of the Preaching Friars."[1] Of late, unfortunate differences have arisen between Mr. Dwane and the Bishop of Grahamstown, who has taken a warm interest in the welfare of the Order, and the Coadjutor-Bishop of Cape Town is now the Acting Provincial. But Mr. Dwane, though no longer the Provincial, is still a member of the Chapter.

Racial feeling is no doubt the primary cause of the Ethiopian movement, but there seems to be no reason to doubt the loyalty of the members of the Order. " I know intimately all the leading members of the Ethiopian Order," wrote another of its former chaplains, the Rev. F. W. Puller, in 1903, "and I can assert from certain knowledge that they are perfectly loyal." And Dr. Cameron, writing in the following year, stated that he knew of no accusation of disloyalty against members of the Order which had stood the test of investigation. "On the other hand," he points out, "at the annual conference of the Order, held in January 1903, a vote of loyalty and congratulation to the King on His Majesty's then recent coronation was spontaneously proposed and passed with acclamation." Although some members of the Order would have preferred a more aggressive policy, Mr. Dwane has endeavoured to avoid undue interference with other religious bodies. His offer to close an Ethiopian chapel at Queenstown on account of its proximity to the S. Andrew's native church, though considerately declined by the vicar, was an instance of his caution in this respect. The members of the Order were described by Dr. Cameron as " invariably respectful to Europeans," and whereas the

[1] See an article in *The Mission Field* of March 1908 on "The Ethiopian Order in South Africa," by the Rev. W. A. Goodwin.

leaders of the A.M.E. Church seem to be in favour of inter-marriage between Europeans and natives, Mr. Dwane is said to be opposed to any such blending of the races. Apparently Mr. Dwane does not seek the position of a political leader. He informed the Native Affairs Commission that he did not encourage his followers to break away from their chiefs, and that personally he took no part in politics, even to the extent of exercising his right to vote. The Order, as a body, would seem to be carrying on religious and educational work without ulterior political motives; it has recognised its need of white supervision; and it has received Government grants for some of its schools. Although the actions of other Ethiopians have probably brought upon it some undeserved discredit, we are not aware that any serious charge has been made good against its members, and there is no justification for placing difficulties in their way so long as their efforts are directed to the true objects of a religious organisation.

When Mr. Dwane and his followers joined the Anglican Church, the acts of Bishop Turner with regard to the union of the Ethiopian Church with the A.M.E. Church had still to be ratified by the latter body. The ratification took place in 1900, and in the following year Bishop Coppin was sent to South Africa to supervise the work of the church in that country. The affiliation of the two churches was thus completed, and thereby the A.M.E. Church secured a definite footing in South Africa. This close connection between the Ethiopians and the negroes of the Southern States is viewed with grave misgiving by many South Africans, who fear that, by stimulating the spirit of racial jealousy and exclusiveness, it may have a sinister influence on the future of South Africa.

The A.M.E. Church owes its origin to a secession in 1787 from the Methodist Society of Philadelphia of its coloured members. The secessionists became an organised body in 1816, and Richard Allen was consecrated as their first bishop. A coloured minister who took part in this secession had been ordained by Bishop White of the Anglican Church of America, a fact which they considered established the validity of their episcopate. While adopting an episcopal organisation, they retained the methodist doctrine. Thus constituted, the church gained numerous adherents. It is estimated that it now has over 5,000 ministers and about 700,000 communicants in America, and that it holds property to the value of about $50,000,000. It has carried on missions in Liberia and Sierra Leone, but apparently it had no immediate intention of undertaking work in South Africa until it was invited to do so by the Ethiopian Church. In South Africa it works as a mission church. About ten or fifteen preachers are assigned to a district, which is placed under the supervision of a presiding elder, and the bishop has to deal with any cases that are considered to require his personal attention. The ministers and presiding elders are appointed by the bishop, who acts in consultation with his presiding elders and leading ministers. In 1903 Bishop Coppin estimated that his church had about 200 ministers in South Africa, including evangelists who had not been ordained, and about 5,000 or 6,000 members. Most of these were in the Transvaal and the Orange River Colony, but as the Governments of these colonies refused Bishop Coppin permission to enter them, he was unable to exercise any effective supervision over this portion of his charge. He visited Rhodesia; but it would appear from the evidence given by his successor, Bishop Smith, before the Native Affairs Commission in 1904 that the A.M.E. Church had then been forbidden to work in that country, and that they were also prohibited from entering Natal, Basutoland, and Bechuanaland. "Therefore," Bishop Smith informed the Commissioners, " so far as those colonies are concerned,

I regard it that our church has ceased to exist, so far
as any direct control or supervision on the part of the
bishop here, or on the part of the bishop at home, is
concerned, thus leaving us with but Cape Colony in
which to operate." The A.M.E. Church can hardly be
held responsible for the conduct of its representatives in
colonies from which its bishop is excluded, except in so
far as the too hasty ordination of some of its ministers
may have caused mischief by placing ill-qualified men in
positions of serious responsibility in those colonies. Some
of these men have no doubt done serious harm to other
religious bodies and to the reputation of their own church,
but the official policy of that church must be judged by its
proceedings in Cape Colony, where its bishop has liberty to
exercise his powers of supervision.

Bishop Coppin assured the Native Affairs Commission
in emphatic terms that his church desired to promote loyalty
to the Governments of the colonies and friendly relations
with the white races. He denied that it contemplated
any scheme for the immigration of negroes from the United
States. He also recognised that much had been done for
the natives in South Africa in providing religious teaching
and education, and in other ways ; and he stated that he
preferred not to obtain members from other churches. No
doubt he was in a position of some difficulty when he came
to South Africa. He was excluded from personal communication with the greater portion of his church ; and
some of his ministers seem to have been quite unfitted
for their duties. He does not, however, appear to have
been very successful in establishing better discipline or a
more healthy spirit amongst his people. He informed the
Native Affairs Commission that he had himself ordained
very few ministers. But he admitted that even these
were not all fit to act as marriage-officers, and amongst
them was William Mokalapa, who subsequently became

notorious for his attempt to wreck M. Coillard's mission in Barotseland. Although Bishop Coppin stated that he was opposed to proselytising from other churches, it would seem that even in Cape Colony he failed to prevent his preachers from doing so. And it must be admitted that their action was hardly unauthorised ; for the extravagant language of the missionary organ of the A.M.E. Church, *The Voice of Missions*, of which Bishop Turner was the editor, was eminently calculated to encourage conduct of this kind. This paper spoke of the day when the natives would "whip" the British "until they reach the banks of the Thames," and urged that foreign missionary associations should consider the best means of transferring their work in Africa "to the society best fitted for the proper and most successful development of it." The aggressions of the A.M.E. Church and suspicions of the loyalty of its members inevitably brought it into grave disrepute in South Africa, and its leaders at length realised that their agents had gone too far. Accordingly, in 1904 a declaration was issued by thirteen bishops, including Bishop Turner, containing the following statements as to the objects of their church :

> In all of our movements in South Africa we shall seek to help and not to hinder ; to assist in advancing enlightened and healthful influences and not to impede them ; to foster and encourage loyalty and obedience to lawfully constituted authority and not to breed disaffection and anarchy.
> In relation to all religious denominations, our position is that of fraternity and co-operation in any and every way that will help to bring the heathen to a knowledge of the true God.
> It is no part of our business to concern ourselves with politics. We shall strictly confine our endeavours to civilisation, education and Christianisation. Our theory in regard to the education of the natives is— the rudiments of an education for all, industrial training for the many, and a college education for the talented few.

Bishop Smith spoke in similar terms before the Native Affairs Commission. He informed the Commissioners that Bishop Turner's "principle of 'Africa for the Africans,' and all that kind of thing, none of us take seriously." He stated also that he regarded proselytising from other churches as "wicked and a waste of time and of men"; and that he noted with regret that some of his ministers had been engaged in undermining the work of old-established missions, as the object of his church was to reach the heathen, not the people who are civilised. It is to be hoped that these views may prevail, and that the A.M.E. Church, by adopting a policy more in accord with its official declarations, may yet find its place in the fellowship of South African churches.

From the time of its arrival in South Africa the A.M.E. Church has given special attention to educational work. It has established a number of schools, of which the most important is the Bethel Institute at Cape Town. At this institution there are about 400 students, and the principal, the Rev. A. H. Attaway, is the head of the educational department of the A.M.E. Church in South Africa, and acted as general superintendent of the Church during Bishop Coppin's absence in America. This institute was referred to in *The Voice of Missions* in bombastic terms, but apparently it has not yet succeeded in complying with the requirements of the Education Department so as to obtain a Government grant. Mr. Attaway, however, takes a thoroughly practical view of the objects of native education. "It is my view in regard to the education of the masses of the natives of the country," he told the Native Affairs Commission, "that, so far as the classes are concerned, they will gradually find their places according to the law of the survival of the fittest and as a matter of selection. And, so far as the masses are concerned, it is my idea, as I have said before, that they ought so to be taught and prepared as to do the manual labour of the country. I believe that if some practical scheme could be placed before them, in order to direct their education in this way, they would accept it and they would do that which is best for them. The native has natural aspirations, but he does not know in many cases really what he requires. He sees the effect of civilisation upon others, and he is very anxious, as far as possible, to keep pace with those things. But, as I see it, his salvation lies in his availability as a labouring asset." Mr. Sargant, in his preliminary report on native education, refers to an attempt which Mr. Attaway was making to establish a village settlement. For this purpose he had purchased a farm in the Western Province of Cape Colony and had built an industrial school ; but the scheme was then still in an initial stage. Besides carrying on schools, the A.M.E. Church has assisted a number of natives, desiring higher education, to go to negro colleges in the United States—a practice which at any rate has had the beneficial effect of stimulating interest in South Africa with regard to the provision of better facilities in that country for the higher education of natives. For financial support, the A.M.E. Church in South Africa depends upon contributions from its members and others, supplemented by funds supplied by its general missionary department in the United States. Small fees are also received from the children in its schools.

Co-operation between its American and South African members has been by no means easy. Often better educated, accustomed to different social conditions, and unfamiliar with South African languages, the American negroes have not always been able to work smoothly with their South African colleagues ; while the latter, although recognising their need of educated men, have endeavoured to check the importation from America of ministers whom they regarded as unfit for work in South Africa.

The A.M.E. Church is not the only organisation of American negroes that has shown an active interest in South Africa. Some years ago the American Baptist Church of coloured people sent the Rev. C. S. Morris to visit South Africa on their behalf. Mr. Morris claimed that during his visit he received into this Baptist Church 1,200 members, representing 17 congregations. This statement is hardly calculated to instil full confidence in the soundness of his methods ; and, like Bishop Turner, he may not have appointed ministers with sufficient regard to their qualifications. Apparently the Church of the Tembus, or the Amatile, as they are sometimes called, mentioned at the beginning of this chapter, have thrown in their lot with this American Baptist Church.

The organisations to which we have referred, with the exception of the American Baptist congregations, owed their origin to secessions from various branches of the Wesleyan Church, but other religious bodies, including even the A.M.E. Church, have not been exempt from similar tendencies. At present most of the seceding bodies are small and comparatively unimportant; but, as they illustrate an important tendency, and their history may throw some light on the difficult question of the position to be accorded to native members in the various churches, it may be worth while to refer briefly to some of the chief of them.

Of all these movements perhaps none has left a more painful memory than the secession from the Lovedale Mission of the United Free Church of Scotland, of which the Rev. P. J. Mzimba was the leader. Mr. Mzimba was educated at Lovedale, and in 1875 he was ordained as a minister. For 22 years he appears to have discharged his duties faithfully. In 1898 he unexpectedly resigned his position. He made no complaint of unjust interference

in his work by the Lovedale authorities or of any lack of
assistance on their part, and the sole reason he gave for his
secession was the desire to act independently of white missionaries. The presbytery considered his case with great
care, but they failed to induce him to reconsider his decision.
He then initiated an independent native church, known as
" The Presbyterian Church of Africa," and issued circulars
to the members of the Free Church in South Africa urging
them to join it. He and his followers also claimed to retain
certain buildings, documents, and money in their possession—a claim which the Free Church successfully disputed.
A large number of natives joined the new church,
including, it is said, two-thirds of the Lovedale congregation; and Mr. Mzimba informed the Native Affairs
Commission in 1903 that it then comprised 6,500 communicants and about 20,000 attenders. He stated that it
was carrying on work in Natal and the Transvaal, as
well as in Cape Colony, and that it had evangelists in the
Orange River Colony and Rhodesia. He also said that
they were working under the Presbyterian system of
Church government ; that they had ordained four ministers ;
that they had established schools; and that some of these
schools had received Government grants, and were supervised by committees of parents, who collected money for
the teachers' salaries. Mr. Mzimba had been elected as
moderator or chairman of the Church Synod, but neither he
nor any of the other ministers had in 1903 been recognised
as marriage-officers. Mr. Mzimba informed the Commission
that he was not associated in any way with the Ethiopian
movement, and added that neither he nor any of his fellow-
ministers had any sympathy with it. He stated that
responsibility stimulated the members of his church in
their work, but he admitted that he was not satisfied with
their progress and expressed a desire for federation with
the white Presbyterians. " I am looking forward to the

time," he said, "which I hope will come, when, while we control our own church matters separately, there will be incorporation or federation with the Colonial Presbyterian body."

Before Mr. Mzimba left the Free Church, there had already been a less serious secession from that body, headed by the Rev. E. Tsewu. Mr. Tsewu also had been educated at Lovedale, and ordained as a Free Church minister, but about nine or ten years ago he and his congregation at Johannesburg, in consequence of some church dispute, left the Free Church, and since that time they have been managing their own affairs as an isolated congregation under the name of "The Independent Native Presbyterian Church." In 1904 they had about 70 communicants, and from 200 to 300 attenders. Mr. Tsewu declared that his secession was not a matter of white versus black; that he did not desire separation; and that he was open to reunion.

Another body of secessionists, known as "The Ethiopian Catholic Church in Zion," were originally members of the Church of England; and their leader, the Rev. S. J. Brander, who received his education at Lovedale, had been ordained as a deacon. Their secession from the Church of England appears to have been due mainly to their desire to have an independent church. At first they joined Mr. Makone and his followers in founding the Church of Ethiopia, and, with them, subsequently became members of the A.M.E. Church. Difficulties, however, soon arose with regard to the financial assistance to be given by that church, and in 1904, after the union had lasted about six years, Mr. Brander and his people again seceded and established the Ethiopian Catholic Church in Zion, with its headquarters at Pretoria. Mr. Brander informed the Native Affairs Commission a few months later that his church then had a membership of over 560 from

Pretoria to Basutoland and British Bechuanaland, with seven ordained ministers, but he stated that he had not yet been recognised as a marriage-officer. He disclaimed any intention of acting as a political leader, and expressed his desire to be under the control of Europeans. " I want them," he said, "as guides over me with all my people."

In Natal Ethiopian tendencies seem to have been stimulated by the wild propaganda of Joseph Booth. In 1896 Mr. Booth, who had been engaged in missionary work in Central Africa, promulgated a scheme to form a joint-stock company of African natives for carrying on the commerce of Africa, and so securing political control.   His motto, "Africa for the Africans," proved attractive to a number of natives, but the scheme came to nothing, owing, it is said, to his hearers' determination to exclude Mr. Booth himself from the management.

There have been two secessions of some importance from the American Zulu Mission—one headed by a preacher at Table Mountain, and the other by a preacher at Johannesburg. These secessions occurred in 1897, and in each case the seceding preacher is said to have taken with him more than half the members of his congregation. The secessionists formed themselves into " The Zulu Congregational Church."   The Table Mountain secession is attributed mainly to the refusal of the preacher to comply with the request of the mission that he should move to some other place. At Johannesburg the native congregation are said to have desired that the preacher should be their head instead of the missionary, and other difficulties arose with regard to the holding of property purchased in part out of money contributed by the natives. In 1898 the seceding ministers, by obtaining ordination in an irregular way, seem to have lost the confidence of some of their followers, and negotiations were opened with the missionaries, which ended in the Johannesburg secessionists re-

joining the mission.   This reunion, however, was only
brought about by " grave but inevitable concessions by
the mission," including " the right to autonomy in accordance with Congregational policy."   The Rev. J. A. Wilder,
D.D., informed the Native Affairs Commission that the
native pastor of the Zulu Congregational Church in
Johannesburg was " a very aggressive man, very intelligent, and very energetic.   He worked all the time, day and
night, and kept five horses going looking after his twenty
stations—which was the work I had left, out-stations and
stations—and that church he had charge of developed from
246, which was the number when I left, to over 600
individual communicants."   Dr. Wilder stated that these
men felt " that the missionaries were keeping back from
them the privilege of running their own churches.   They
had not the least idea of any interference with the Government ; there was not the least political thought, so far as
our people were concerned."

In Natal there have also been secessions from the Free
Church of Scotland, the Gordon Memorial Mission, and
the Wesleyans.   Some of the secessionists have formed
an organisation known as the " Uhlanga Church " (the
National Church), which apparently does not bear a high
reputation.   Some followers of the Rev. — Mbiyana, who
seceded from the American Mission about twenty-five
years ago, are said to remain in the Noodsberg district ;
certain natives near the coast, calling themselves " Ethiopians," have their headquarters in Durban ; and in the
south of the Colony there is a body, connected with the
American Coloured Baptist Church, whose members call
themselves the " Amakusha " (Cushites).   In the docks
location at Cape Town there have been natives belonging
to the Apostolic Holiness Communion ; and no doubt
other native churches or religious societies might be
enumerated.   Those which have been specifically men-

tioned represent, however, the main developments of the Ethiopian movement, and the nature of that movement can be gathered from the circumstances of their origin and the character of their work.

Apparently none of these secessions have been due to doctrinal differences, for the secessionists have generally, if not always, retained, at any rate for a time, the theological views of their parent church. Sometimes the immediate cause of secession has been little more than a matter of personal incompatibility. Friction has arisen between some native minister and the white missionary, and the former, to escape from what he regarded as undue interference from the missionary, has left the mission, set up a church of his own, and has been joined by other native members. The missionary naturally regards this conduct as ungrateful and disloyal, and witnesses the loss of his converts with something like dismay. But a closer investigation shows that there is more in the movement than this personal aspect. Its real significance lies in its racial character. The idea of a tribal church embodied in the "Church of the Tembus," founded by Nehemiah Tile, has developed into a far wider conception, revealing a new and growing sense of national life. "The idea of secession," says Mr. Sargant in his report on native education, "is probably not due only, or primarily, to a wish on the part of the native leaders to manage their ecclesiastical affairs for themselves, but also to a real longing for national union through a single spiritual head of the church"; and he points out that, owing to the distinctions of tribe and language by which the natives are divided, it was natural that this national feeling should find its first expression through Christianity. Similar views are expressed by the Rev. F. B. Bridgman in a paper on the Ethiopian Movement read before the Missionary Conference in Natal. "The fact," he says, "that a

great race, hitherto content to grovel, has at last begun
to aspire is momentous." And the Coadjutor-Bishop of
Cape Town, who, as chaplain to the Order of Ethiopia,
had special opportunities for observing the inner working
and spirit of the movement, declares emphatically that
its "root-principle is, I believe, patriotism; in other
words, the self-assertion of a growing national life." To
this sudden and unexpected awakening of racial aspirations must be attributed the rapid development of the
movement, which has so disquieted the white community,
and seems to have astonished no one more than the missionaries, who were unintentionally responsible for it. It
is, perhaps, surprising that so able a body of men as the
leading South African missionaries, with their long and
intimate experience of native affairs, should in this instance have failed so signally to read the signs of the
times. Had they gauged the position more accurately,
it is conceivable that they might have been able to
direct the movement into safer channels, and to have
averted painful breaches between native churches and
their parent missions. But the workings of the native
mind have often proved inscrutable to the white man.
Many of these missionaries are at any rate doing their
utmost to remedy their mistake. If at first they were
dismayed at the apparently ruthless wrecking of their
missions by natives whom they had trained and trusted,
they are now facing the new conditions with singular
devotion and in a statesmanlike spirit. Setting aside
their personal feelings, they have endeavoured to do
justice to the aims of the secessionists, and have sought
to promote what is best in the movement, while re-
straining its abuses and extravagances. The Conference of Missionaries at Johannesburg in 1904 refused
to court popularity by passing any resolution hostile
to the establishment of independent native churches,

and insisted on the need of guidance rather than of repression.   Missionaries indeed recognise that the establishment of such churches is the ultimate object of their work,
and there is a strong feeling that some distinction between
European and native churches is desirable in the best
interests of both.   But at present it seems clear that
sympathetic supervision by a white missionary or minister
is generally essential to the healthy progress of a native
church ; and the premature rejection by the extreme
Ethiopian bodies of this supervision has caused serious
injury both to themselves and to other churches.

The missionaries have to face a twofold problem.   On
the one hand, they have to determine how best they may
promote friendly relations with the independent native
churches, and, if possible, guide their action by wise
counsels and personal influence ; and, on the other, they
have to consider what policy they should adopt towards
the native ministers and members of their own missions
and churches in order to give these natives scope for their
legitimate aspirations.   Any attempts to influence the
action of the native churches necessarily call for the exercise of great tact on the part of the missionaries.   In these
churches racial feeling is strong, and the desire to show
that natives are capable of managing their own ecclesiastical affairs makes them exceedingly sensitive with
regard to any interference by white missionaries.   Nevertheless, it is evident that these natives are beginning to
understand that their independence has involved them in
many difficulties with which they are not yet fitted to
cope.   There are signs that some at least of them recognise
their need of help and guidance.   " We find we want
some one to help us ; we cannot get on by ourselves," was
the explanation given to the Bishop of Pretoria by the
representatives of a body of about a thousand Ethiopians
who had applied to him for admission into the Church of

England ; and in matters of finance and church discipline particularly this need is no doubt often keenly felt. There is reason, therefore, to hope that, if the secessionists are convinced that the missionaries have a genuine and disinterested concern for the welfare of the native churches, some of them may be glad to welcome a missionary in the rôle of friendly adviser.

On the whole, this impression is confirmed by the results of the first efforts of the missionaries to establish better relations with the independent native churches. In July 1904 the Conference of Missionaries at Johannesburg addressed carefully considered representations to the heads of the American negro denominations with reference to certain acts of these denominations which constituted the chief obstacles to co-operation between them and the European missionaries. In these representations the Conference referred to the " ultimate self-support, self-control, and self-propagation " of the native churches as " the recognised goal of mission work," and admitted that the political aspect of Ethiopianism might have been exaggerated. But it deplored the tendency of the Ethiopian bodies to proselytise in fields occupied by other churches, their ordination of men unfit for the ministry, their lax discipline, their encouragement of schism, and the emphasis laid by them on distinctions of colour. The first response to this action by the missionaries came from the Ethiopians in the Transvaal and Orange River Colony, who had joined the A.M.E. Church, but over whom, it must be remembered, that church had little or no official control. These natives held a conference in Pretoria in August 1904, at which, after indulging in abusive references to some of the missionaries, they passed resolutions repudiating the accusations of lax discipline and encouragement of schism, and declaring that they viewed with distrust and had lost

confidence in the cause represented by the majority of the
members of the Johannesburg conference. They expressed
their thanks, however, to the Bishop of Lebombo and the
Rev. E. Jacottet and a few others for "their true missionary
spirit." M. Jacottet, who had read a paper at the conference on the native churches and their organisation, took
the opportunity thus offered him to address an open letter
of friendly advice to the assistant-secretary of the Ethiopian
conference, in which, after refusing to be dissociated from
his fellow missionaries, he protested against the unfriendly
attitude adopted by. the A.M.E. Church, and dealt
faithfully with the shortcomings of that body, explaining
that, while the missionaries desired to co-operate with the
native churches, they were unable to do so until the
practices to which they had referred were abandoned. At
this stage Bishop Smith, who had just arrived in South
Africa, intervened in the controversy. In a brief reply
to M. Jacottet's letter, he disowned "the intemperate and
unchristian language" of the Pretoria conference, and
requested M. Jacottet to supply him with a number of
copies of his letter to send to the bishops and general
officers of his church in America, describing it as "a most
excellent pamphlet." These incidents show at least that
advice from white missionaries, if tendered in a sympathetic
spirit, is not always resented by the leaders of native
churches, and they illustrate the nature of the new
relations that are growing up between these organisations
and the white missions. It is to be hoped that the
missionaries will lose no opportunity of showing their
interest in the progress of the new churches and of
winning the confidence of their members, for in hardly
any other way can they do greater service to the cause
of racial amity or more effectively promote the true objects
of their work.

The various churches have endeavoured to solve the

problem of the status of native members in different ways. The Trappists, Jesuits, Marists, and other Roman Catholic missionaries, keep their native converts in a subordinate position, enforcing a strict discipline and insisting on industrial training. " I noticed in the church of the splendid Trappist mission in Natal," writes Mr. A. Colquhoun,[1] " that the members of the Order, the lay brothers, and the native congregation, each had their special place in which they worshipped "; and he points out that, although a native may sometimes become a lay brother, the Roman Catholic bodies "admit no natives to their orders, and maintain a strictly disciplinarian relation with all their converts, never admitting them to an equality in matters ecclesiastical." To this policy he attributes their comparative immunity from Ethiopian secession. The Protestant churches, on the other hand, aim at training their native members in the management of church affairs, and encourage them to take an active part in spreading Christianity among their own people. White and native members usually meet in separate congregations, but natives are appointed as catechists, evangelists, and elders, and are even ordained as ministers and admitted to the governing bodies of those churches.

The episcopal system of the Church of England enables that church to exercise supervision over its native congregations, while allowing them, as in the case of the Order of Ethiopia, to undertake considerable responsibilities; and it is probably due, at least in part, to this episcopal supervision that the Church of England has escaped Ethiopian secessions on a serious scale. The relations between the white and the native members of the church have, however, still to be determined. The Bishop of Pretoria informed the Native Affairs Commission that a special commission had been appointed

[1] In his book entitled " In Africander Land."

to investigate this subject; and he suggested that the solution might be found in the establishment of separate European and native churches, "both bound to and governed by the Provincial Synod," in which the natives, as well as the whites, would be represented, but with some safeguard to protect the interests of the whites in view of the overwhelming numbers of the natives. The Coadjutor-Bishop of Cape Town states[1] that many of the leading clergy in South Africa are in favour of separate church organisations for whites and natives; and he points out that this policy would remove many difficulties which exist under the present system. A minister or missionary who is well fitted to work among colonists may not be qualified for work among natives. At church synods and con-ferences many questions of importance to the whites are hardly intelligible to the natives; and, on the other hand, matters which may be vital to the natives are often not understood by the whites. There is some anxiety also as to whether the native clergy are sufficiently independent and free from tribal and personal considerations to take part on the same footing as their white brethren in so responsible a matter as the election of a bishop. Dr. Cameron suggests, therefore, that it might be better for the native clergy to elect their own bishop, subject to the veto of the native representative laity, and that their bishop should be a coadjutor to the bishop of the diocese, or possibly to more than one diocesan. "The bond of unity," he points out, "would remain in the Archbishop and the diocesan Episcopate and the Provincial Synod, in which both European and native diocesan synods might be represented."

An instructive object-lesson in methods of church organi-

[1] In the article on the Ethiopian Movement and the Order of Ethiopia in *The East and the West* (October 1904, p. 391) already referred to.

sation is provided by the Paris Evangelical Mission Society in Basutoland.   The native church which this Society has established, known as the Church of Basutoland, contained 40,956 adherents according to the census of 1904, and its title shows the desire of the Society that it should become the national church of the Basuto.   The policy of the Society accordingly is to develop to the utmost the capacity of the native members to undertake responsible duties. The church organisation consists of the Seboka or Assembly, the Conference of European Missionaries, the Synod, and the Consistories.   The Seboka has been composed of sixteen European missionaries and nine native ministers, and four more native ministers were to have been added to it in 1907. It decides all matters affecting the life of the church, except the status of missionaries and the districts in which they are to work.   It also supervises the primary schools of the church through its Education Board, consisting of a secretary of schools, three missionaries, and a native minister. The Conference of Missionaries deals with the administration of funds received from Europe, with secondary and industrial education, and with the missionaries' personal affairs.   The Synod is an advisory body meeting every two years, and consists of about 100 members, comprising the missionaries and native ministers and delegates from the various parishes. It is intended that the Synod should ultimately relieve the home Society of its responsibility for the general work of the church.   Below these bodies there is in each parish a consistory for the management of parochial affairs.   It comprises the local missionary or native minister, who acts as president, the catechists, and elders elected by the Christian members of the station and out-stations from a list prepared by the missionary and his consistory.   Mr. Sargant points out that its procedure is modelled on the Sesuto custom of the chief in khotla : the proceedings begin with a general discussion, and the president then announces his decision, in which he usually follows the general opinion of the consistory.[1]

How much may be gained by entrusting positions of responsibility in this way to carefully chosen and thoroughly trained natives may be gathered from the following account by the Rev. E. Jacottet of the practical working of this system of church government. "It is said every day in South African and English newspapers," M. Jacottet writes,[2] "that they (*i.e.* the South African natives) are children and ought to be treated as children. Whilst this opinion may be true as far as the bulk of the heathen population is concerned—and even then not without qualifications—it is no more true of the large part of the Christianised population. They have advanced very quickly and in a remarkable way during the last ten or twenty years, and a large number of them have already given proofs of high qualifications which give them the right to be considered as being no more children, but grown-up men, able to hold their own in the world, and who should be treated as such.

"We have practical proof of that in our mission, and the policy we have adopted for some years of giving to our churches, and especially to our native ministers, a great amount of self-government, and of trusting them, has been an undoubted success. After having felt our way for a certain time with our first native ministers, not knowing exactly what special rights we should give them, we decided in 1898 to trust them entirely, and to take them into our councils on terms of equality with ourselves. We had then three fully qualified (ordained) native ministers ; we have nine of them now, and next year their number will

---

[1] See Mr. E. B. Sargant's description of the organisation of the Church of Basutoland in his *Report on Education in Basutoland*, 1905-6, p. 142 *et seq.* (Longmans, Green & Co.)

[2] In a letter to this Committee dated July 28, 1906.

have risen to thirteen. Our decision, which may have—
in fact, has—seemed rash to some of our best friends, has
proved itself to have been, not only liberal, but very wise,
and even those of our number who would have criticised it
at the time, are quite content with it now. Indeed, I don't
think that one of us would ever think of discussing it now.
It is very likely this that has prevented Ethiopianism from
making any headway in Basutoland, and from harming in
any way our churches. We have had no secessions to
speak of; all our staff, all our congregations have never
wavered for a minute in their allegiance to our church.

" Since the year 1898 the governing body of our church
is composed of the white missionaries (18 in number)
and the native ministers (9 in number now, 13 next
year). This Conference directs all the church affairs,
controls the finances of the church, the schools, etc. In it
the native ministers have exactly the same voting power
and rights as the white missionaries. Its discussions are
conducted in the native language, which all our missionaries
are expected to speak, and in fact do speak. The plan has
answered uncommonly well, and there has never appeared
any racial feeling, even when we had to discuss questions
which might easily have led to it. Our native ministers
have not been slow to recognise that we had given them
their full rights, and that in working with us for the benefit
of their tribe they will do more and better work than in
separating from us to join any Ethiopian body. They
know that we want to educate them—and through them the
rest of the church—to self-government, that we want to
increase their influence year after year, and that we do not
desire to impose our own views and ways upon them. We
want them to become ultimately their own masters in their
own church. It may still take some time ; but we are far
more advanced than we should have believed it probable
some years ago. Our theological school has now become

a permanent institution, after having been only tentative for some years; and in a few years the native ministers will have an undoubted majority in our conference. We are not afraid of the prospect; we know that they will be wise enough to go on upon the same lines, and to understand that it is their interest, and the interest of their church, to trust us and to work with us. They know that we have only their interest at heart, that we only want them to progress and to develop; they trust us, and will for ever be thankful to our mission for what it has done for them.

"Each one of our native ministers is placed at the head of one parish, where he is nearly in everything just as independent as a European missionary. We have now fourteen parishes directed by European missionaries, and nine directed by native ministers. We decided at our last con-ference upon the creation of three new parishes for native ministers, and next year we may probably decide upon the creation of another one, so that we shall have thirteen parishes with native ministers, against fourteen with European missionaries. In a few years' time the parishes directed by native ministers will be more numerous than the others, as the number of native ministers will increase, whereas our own staff will not, even if it may not eventually be reduced.

"As stated above, the native minister has, in his own parish, the full rights of a minister, administering the funds, baptizing, organising, etc., subject, of course, as every one, to the general constitution of the church. The only difference from the European missionary is this: he is given one of the European missionaries as his special adviser in difficult cases. But this does not make him a minor or inferior. In practice he is just as free as I am myself in my own parish. And, instead of resenting it, our native ministers are glad to know that they have somebody to help them with his advice in their difficulties. From what I have seen myself personally, and from what I hear from *all* my colleagues, the system works exceedingly well, and in the administration of their parishes and their ecclesiastical and educational work our native ministers are not a bit behind their European brethren. They may lack something in administrative faculties, but they have a stronger hold upon the people and are wonderfully respected by them. It is, as I said, an undoubted success, and I would urge every mission to follow the same road.

" I should add that we have been very careful in choosing and in educating our staff. We only receive into our theological school men who have been at work as teachers or evangelists for some years and whose character has been tried. They must also have a fair amount of knowledge, and have passed at least the third year's pupil teachers' examination of the Cape Colony. They must then pass through a three years' course of study ; and, when they have finished their studies, they have again to be tried for one or two years in the service of the church before being ordained."

The Church of England has adopted a somewhat similar policy in Basutoland.[1] Its work in that country is divided into seven districts ; a mission priest is placed in charge of each district; and he is assisted by an Advisory Church Council of natives. These councils appoint representatives to a Missionary Conference presided over by the Bishop of Bloemfontein. There are only about twelve white members of this Conference, to which twelve native representatives (all laymen) are sent from Basutoland alone. Its functions are advisory only, but although its resolutions do not bind the Bishop, he usually acts in accordance with them : and, if thought desirable, a resolution of this Conference may be laid before the Diocesan Synod, and may then go forward to the Pro-

[1] See Mr. E. B. Sargant's Report on Education in Basutoland, p. 168.

vincial Synod for South Africa, and finally to the Conference of Colonial Bishops at Lambeth.

Natives are also admitted to the governing body of the Wesleyan Church in South Africa.[1] The General Conference of this church is constituted of certain European official members, with two white and two native ministers and two white and two native laymen. Under this General Conference there are separate synod meetings of the native ministers and European missionaries. This system is also said to work satisfactorily. The Wesleyans, Congregationalists, and Presbyterians hold that all ministers must stand on an equal footing, without distinction of colour ; and, in the absence of any episcopal authority, it is a somewhat difficult matter in these churches to provide the supervision which is needed by native congregations. It seems clear that, at any rate for the present, the supervision of the native churches must mainly devolve on the missionaries ; and they will need exceptional discretion and tact to perform this duty efficiently without giving offence to their native colleagues. Their hope of success lies in the natives' need of guidance, especially perhaps in matters of finance. "A more difficult and spiritual service," says the Rev. F. B. Bridgman in the paper on Ethiopianism already referred to, "never has the missionary in this field been called upon to render. For the helpfulness of such service the native Christian is ready and sometimes anxious." It may be open to question whether the congregational system adopted by some denominations is well adapted for a native church. It does not seem to fit in very well with the natives' ideas of tribal authority, and probably tends to produce laxity of discipline. It might therefore be worth while for these churches to consider whether they would not work more effectively in South

[1] See the evidence of the Rev. J. Scott before the South African Native Affairs Commission, 1903-5.

Africa if they modified their constitution in order to provide some adequate central authority, representative both of their white and native members.

The general principles which should govern the organisation of a native church were considered with great care in a paper read by the Rev. E. Jacottet at the missionary conference at Johannesburg in 1904. He advised that there should be complete separation between the European and native churches ; that a certain amount of autonomy should be given to tribal or racial units within the church ; that the governing body should be "*distinctly native*," carrying on its discussions in the language of the natives ; that the church should be self-supporting ; that native ministers should be thoroughly trained, but not on lines calculated to put them out of sympathy with their people, and that they should be ordained and supported by the native church ; also that the missionary should be supported from home and should continue to supervise the church only so long as his guidance is needed. In M. Jacottet's opinion, the native ministers and lay delegates on the governing body of the native church should have the same rights and voting power as the European missionaries, who on such a body would be acting simply as ministers. " Some may think it dangerous," he writes. " I do not believe it to be so. The superior insight and education of the European missionary, his riper Christian character, will give him a great personal influence, which shall be only greater when it does not rest upon mere rights. The native ministers are sure to trust him when they see and feel that all his sympathies are with them. Personal experience has taught me that we may safely trust our native colleagues with such rights and powers." M. Jacottet admits that he is an optimist, and that others do not share to the full his confidence in the Christian native ; but an optimism that has survived the disillusions of a long missionary career is probably not without some justification. Missionaries who approach the question of Ethiopianism in this judicial spirit are rendering a public service of great value. For it is evident that many Colonists are very imperfectly informed with regard to these matters, and view them with a good deal of prejudice. Baseless accusations are too often brought against Ethiopian leaders, and their objects are often misunderstood and misrepresented. The opinion is widely held that native churches are little more than political associations under a thin ecclesiastical disguise, and that their essential purpose is, not to preach Christianity, but to spread the propaganda of " Africa for the Africans." These views do not seem to be justified. Nevertheless, it must be acknowledged that the exaggerated importance which has been attached to the political aspects of the movement is largely due to the mischievous, if not disloyal and seditious, language of which some of the Ethiopians have apparently been guilty. And the growth of the native churches certainly has an important political aspect. A large proportion of the most intelligent and best educated natives are to be found among the ministers and members of these churches, and many of them are keenly interested in politics, especially from the racial standpoint. The native is accustomed to the discussion of tribal affairs ; he has considerable gifts of debate ; and politics have a strong attraction for him. The members of the native churches are not likely therefore to hold aloof from political questions ; and their experience in organising themselves for ecclesiastical purposes no doubt makes it easier for them to overcome tribal differences and to form political associations. Bodies of this kind are already being established, and it is not yet possible to speak with confidence as to their influence and objects. Still it seems clear that the political tendencies of Ethiopianism are its inevitable consequences rather than its cause ; and the missionaries, who are in the best position to judge, and have studied the movement most carefully, are inclined to admit that the importance of its political side has been overestimated. The most authoritative official view of the movement is contained in the report of the Native Affairs Commission of 1903–5. The Commissioners described the movement as " the outcome of a desire on the part of the natives for ecclesiastical self-support and self-control, first taking tangible form in the secession of discontented and restless spirits from religious bodies under the supervision of European missionaries without any previous external incitation thereto." And the Commission reported that it "is not disposed to condemn the aspiration after religious independence, unassociated with mischievous political propaganda, but at the same time does not fail to recognise that in the case of a subject race such an aspiration misdirected on the one hand by the leadership of ignorant and misguided men and repressed by misunderstanding or harshness on the other might be fraught with the seeds of racial mistrust and discontent." The Commission, how-ever, "would not advise any measure of legislative repression, unless unforeseen developments render it necessary, considering that effort should rather be directed towards securing efficient constitutional control and organis-ation in order that the influences at work may be wisely directed, and any individual cases in which pastors abuse the trust reposed in them, may be amenable to authoritative discipline. To this end the Commission would deprecate the recognition of detached secessionary fragments acknow-ledging no efficient central authority." In the opinion of the Commissioners, recognition should be accorded " to such native churches as are possessed of sufficiently stable organisation to control their pastors and enforce discipline where necessary and to ensure the appointment to the

ministry of reliable and worthy men only"; but encouragement should not be given to "those bodies which owe
their existence to the discontent, or, as in some cases, to
the very misconduct of men who, with a following of
kindred spirits, have severed connection with their parent
church, and own no competent central authority." In
pursuance of this policy, the Commissioners recommend
that "no minister shall solemnise marriages without being
licensed as a marriage-officer"; and they express the
opinion that by "a judicious exercise of the right to withhold such licences" the Government would be able to
differentiate between the religious organisations which
were working satisfactorily and those which were not. In
this way the Commissioners hoped that "what is worthless
and unstable in the movement will dwindle into insignifi-
cance, while so much of it as is lasting and in harmony
with the true principles of religious and social advancement will not be unduly impeded, but will grow in the
fulness of time to be a power for good"; a hope which
we share.

CHAPTER VIII

CONCLUSIONS

THIS book has shown, it is hoped, that for the natives of South Africa the old order is giving place to a new order, and that the change is going on rapidly. Chief among the changes—and one which must be productive of others—is the fact that most able-bodied young natives leave their homes for longer or shorter periods of employment elsewhere. This in itself means a change in the native which it would be hard to overrate. The young native does not go out to work as a permanent wage-earner. He usually returns home after a comparatively short term of remunerative employment, bringing with him a new sense of independence and a desire to improve his lot. Too often, however, he also acquires a taste for the vices of the debased European, which are alien to the morality of his tribe. Thus the effect of his employment is to put him out of touch not only with the unprogressive and degrading side of the tribal polity, but also with its wholesome discipline and restraints. In both directions, therefore, the economic change is disintegrating the tribal society, and is depriving the native of his old moral standards. It is this that makes of such vital importance the treatment of the native labourer while working for the white man and his protection from vicious influences. If he acquired a standard of individual responsibility, his new repugnance to the communal responsibility

227

and tribal obedience, which are the foundations of social existence in his tribe, would not be so disastrous.

Unfortunately, the old moral order departs without a new moral order taking its place. The annual reports of the magistrates are full of statements as to the insubordination of the young men returned from work. In reporting on the crimes during the year 1904 one magistrate remarks: "The culprits are principally from what may be termed the rising generation. What one notices more than anything else is the want of responsibility and trust amongst the younger people." An old and trusted chief, eighty years old (1905), complained that "our sons elbow us away from the boiled mealies in the pot when we reach for a handful to eat, saying, 'We bought these, father.'" This new spirit of independence has already produced a widespread feeling of unrest and change. It must be guided in the direction of progress, and not allowed to lead to general lawlessness.

There are many instances in the official reports of what can be achieved by such guidance and of the mischief which arises from its absence. In Natal a poll-tax was imposed in 1906 upon all who did not already pay hut-tax. This new tax fell upon the young men who had hitherto escaped direct taxation, except in so far as they contributed to the hut-tax of the head of their family. The resentment shown by the young natives amounted in some districts to open insubordination and defiance, so much so that the imposition of this poll-tax was referred to at the time as possibly one of the causes of the native rising of that year. In Rhodesia, on the other hand, the youths seem actually to have welcomed such a tax as a recognition and sign of their manhood and independence.

In every way contact with the white man has some disintegrating effect on native society. It is incumbent on him to see that his influence is not destructive only. He ought not, for his own immediate gain, to leave nothing but ruin behind him. He should do his utmost to direct into right paths the force which he is unloosing. The native has inherited a law-abiding instinct. It is therefore all the more deplorable when this is allowed to be broken down. The change, already rapid, will quicken. In a few years many will have fallen away from the tribal organisation; and the broken units of a tribe do not become so many capable individuals. There remains the task of carrying over into a new civilisation the disbanded members of an older and simpler organisation.

The awakened energy of the native shows itself in many ways. He falls a ready victim to vicious influences, but he appreciates and eagerly seeks the benefits of education. Here again he is in danger of receiving what is ill-fitted to his needs. There is little doubt that serious mischief has been done by unwise educational methods.

What, then, are the avenues along which the white man can lead these millions of natives so dependent upon him? One thing is clear. The results achieved by the missionaries of the various churches show that by religious and moral training and education adapted to his needs and capacities, the native can be fitted to fill a place of great usefulness in the community. He can be raised to higher levels of living. He can be disciplined in habits of independence and self-control. But the work of the missionaries needs general recognition and support. And the necessary incentives to progress should be offered to the native in no grudging spirit. The native who wins his way from the kraal to positions of responsibility and trust should not find his path beset with obstacles. If he shows himself able and willing to become a useful citizen, it should be made easy for him to do so and to train his children to follow his example.

How far are these conditions realised? In Cape Colony

the native has an open door. He can buy land ; he can qualify for the franchise on the same terms as the white man. Apparently he can legally become a member of the Legislative Assembly. There are certain laws (*e.g.* the Liquor Laws) which apply only to natives. But for most purposes the native in the Colony proper has practically the same civil and political rights as the white man. In Natal the purchase of land by a native is permitted. But it is difficult for him to obtain exemption from native law, and practically impossible to become a voter.[1] In the Transvaal he can hold land and can obtain exemption from native law, but he has no political rights. In the Orange River Colony he cannot buy or lease land ; he has no political rights ; and, unless he is a minister or teacher, he cannot get exemption from native law.

To what extent the natives should receive political rights is a question which South Africa must determine for herself. But something should be done to meet the higher wants and satisfy the aspirations of those who are now a disturbing element. In Cape Colony some attempts are made to meet their needs and provide an outlet for their energy by the gradual extension of district councils, by the encouragement of education, and by the intro-duction of individual tenure of land. In Natal, on the other hand, the question seems hardly to have been taken up in any practical or far-sighted manner. From the report of the Commission (1907) it seems clear that a policy must be laid down which shall deal with such questions as congestion, uncertainty of tenure and of boundaries, excessive burdens arising from rents or interest on money borrowed. These and many other grievances lie at the bottom of the native unrest which this, " the oldest colony in South Africa," has found herself compelled to crush with an iron hand during the last two years.

[1] Only two or three natives have been given the franchise in Natal.

Another fact is to be recognised. The mass of the natives are, and must long remain, an agricultural people. It is essential, therefore, for their future development, that ample land should be reserved for their use, and every possible effort should be made to teach and encourage them to improve their methods of cultivation. This is the natural and healthy direction for native progress to take. When they are ready for emancipation from the tribal system, opportunities should be freely afforded them of becoming farmers or cultivators on their own account. As the native agriculturist becomes more efficient and better educated, his growing requirements will not only make him personally more thrifty and industrious, but will provide openings for other natives as more or less skilled artisans. Instruction in agriculture needs, therefore, to be supplemented by industrial training. In the future many natives should find occupation among their own people, as well as among the whites, as carpenters, builders, and blacksmiths, and in similar capacities.

Unfortunately there has been no purpose common to all the colonies in the education of the native to take some predetermined place in the body politic or even in the industrial ranks of the community. What education he has got in the past has been in the main only provided by many missionary societies, each working in its own way. Grafted on to this, the prevalent spirit of independence has given rise to political organisations and a native press, and has produced the widespread Ethiopian movement. Everywhere guidance and control are required rather than repression. In all the provision for education there is need of adaptation to the life and future requirements of the native.

The questions of administration, taxation, and franchise also will have to be faced in this spirit. At present, at all points there is felt to be an antagonism between the interests of whites and natives. They are not working for a common end. How can a stable State be built on such a foundation ? The aim must be to find some constructive policy, some check upon the demoralisation which follows so easily and unhappily contact between the two races. It is universally admitted that the natives, where properly led, have shown themselves in the past truthful and law-abiding. Individuals among them, including some of the great chiefs, are capable of understanding very high standards both of loyalty and of administration. These qualities it must be the policy to develop and restore, so that, at any rate, the best of the natives may feel that both races are working to a common end. Several important Commissions have sat, and much information has been gathered, showing clearly whither the old policy has led. The white man has had what he asked for. He has broken the lazy quiet of the native, and induced him to come out and work for him. He has taught him incidentally much that clashes with his life at home. He has made that life impossible. The Colonists often complain that those who are concerned for the interests of the natives are unable to appreciate the vital importance of keeping a firm hand over them. Yet the future of the colonies must be seriously imperilled if there is much further delay in substituting a real scheme of progress for the present destruction of native tribal traditions.

To frame a policy suitable for the new and unstable conditions of the native communities is no easy task. The detribalised and educated natives—now fast increasing in number—will more and more have to be considered. The growing influence of the native press must be reckoned with. Scope will have to be allowed for the legitimate ambitions of the natives. The true safety against wild schemes will be in outlets for reasonable aspirations. To keep wide open the door of hope is essential to a wise policy. It is true that the policy of the future will need to be firm, but it will also need to be consistent and studious of native interests. Above all, it should be based on a clearer conception than at present exists of the true relations between the two races. This may have to be reached by the long pathway of experience and experiment. But at least it is possible to recognise the direction and spirit in which it should be sought. The Colonist himself often describes this relationship as one of guardian and ward. However incomplete this conception may be, we do not doubt the sincerity of those who adopt it. In the work of the Commissions on Native Affairs we have a detailed scrutiny of the extent to which the duties of guardianship and trust are performed. Can it be said that the guardians or trustees have seen to the education of those for whom they act? Have they avoided squandering or wasting the estate of their ward? In the account which they render of their stewardship, do they show that they have acted for the best for their ward, and have not exploited him for their own purposes? These tests could hardly be satisfied by the policy of the past. Will the policy of the future conform to them? In this book facts are told which make the outlook hopeful.

STATUTES, ORDINANCES, PROCLAMATIONS, ETC.

CAPE COLONY

NATAL

THE TRANSVAAL

THE ORANGE RIVER COLONY

SOUTHERN RHODESIA

NORTH-WESTERN RHODESIA

NORTH-EASTERN RHODESIA

BECHUANALAND PROTECTORATE

INDEX

Aborigines, training schools for teachers, 144

Adams, Dr., of the American Zulu Mission, 149

Addison, R. H., on the effect of the poll-tax in Natal, 92, 93

Administration, general features, 98–101 ; existing laws and administrative systems, 101–7 ; jurisdiction and duties of European officers and native chiefs, 108–10 ; councils as an aid to, 110–13 ; the future, 113–20, 231–3

Adviser, Native, in Orange River Colony, 105

African Methodist Episcopalian Church, 145, 162, 168, 169, 194, 195, 197, 199–205, 207, 213, 214; *The Voice of Missions*, 202, 203

Agriculture. *See* Natives and Land Tenure

Allen, Richard, first Bishop of the African Methodist Episcopalian Church, 200

Amakola natives, 150 *n.*

Amakusha, 209

Amanzimtote Institution, 149

Amazansi natives, 18

American Board of Missions, its Zulu Mission, 149, 173, 208, 209

American Coloured Baptist Church, 205

American Methodist Church in Rhodesia, 173

Anglican Church. *See* Church of England

Apostolic Holiness Communion, 209

Appleyard, Rev. W., translator of Kafir Bible, 142

Arbousset, M., 155

Artisans, 39, 231

Ashton, Mr., 139

Asiatics in South Africa (*see also* Chinese), 7

Attaway, Rev. A. H., African Methodist Episcopalian Church, 203, 204

Bantu natives. *See* Natives

Baptists. *See* American

Barnes, G. W., on natives at Kimberley, 36

Barnett, P. A., Director of Education in Natal, on native servants, 187

Bastards, 126, 127

Basutoland, area and population of, 7, 98 ; European goods purchased by natives, 11, 87 ; agricultural stock of natives, 11 ; recruiting for mines, 29, 30 ; labour passes, 167 *n.* ; native artisans, 39 ; land tenure, 71 ; hut-tax, 82–4 ; customs duties, 87 ; licence fees, 89 ; expenses of administration borne by natives, 91 ; administrative system and jurisdiction of chiefs, 106–9 ; council of, 112–3 ; operation of native law, 130 ; marriage law, 132 ; Paris Evangelical and other missions, 155–62 ; native education, *see* Education ; small progress of Ethiopianism, 219 ; Church of Basutoland, 157, 217–21

Bechuanaland Protectorate, The, area and population of, 7, 98 ; natives employed on Transvaal mines, 29, 30 ; land tenure, 70–1, 72 *n.* ; hut-tax, 83 ; increase of hut-tax, 85 ; administrative system and jurisdiction of chiefs, 99, 106–9 ; definition of " Native," 127 ; missions in, 139, 176 ; native education, *see* Education ; native churches, 176

Berlin Missionary Society, 142, 167, 168, 170, 171, 172

Bethel Institute, The, in Capetown, 145, 203

Bloemfontein, native artisans, 39, 158 ; native location at, 70 ; diocese of, 140

Blythswood Institution, 140, 146

Booth, Joseph, 208

Boyce, Rev. W., Kafir grammar, 142

Brander, Rev. S. J., 207

Bridgman, Rev. F. B., the Ethiopian Movement, 192 *n.*, 210, 222

British Central Africa, recruiting in, 28, 29, 31

Brownlee, W. T., on farming, 20 ; on treatment of natives, 26 ; on individual tenure, 60

Butterworth district, individual tenure, 58, 59, 60

Callaway, Dr., first Bishop of St. John's, 140

Cameron, Rev. W. W., Coadjutor-Bishop of Capetown, on the Order of Ethiopia and native churches, 192 *n.*, 197, 198, 216

Cape Colony (*see also* Transkeian Territories), area and population of, 7, 98 ; occupations of

natives and other coloured people, 6–10 ; wages of natives, *see* Wages ; farm labour, 13–8 ; natives selling wool, 11 ; coloured and native farmers and owners of land, 18–20, 57–8, 76–8 ; natives on diamond mines, 35–6 ; natives employed in Transvaal mines, 26, 29, 30, 32 ; natives on coal mines, 36–7 ; dock labourers, 37, 40 ; railway employees, 37–8 ; natives in postal service, 38 ; domestic servants, 38 ; communal tenure of land, 52–3 ; locations, *see* Reserves and Locations ; individual tenure, 52, 58–61, 111, 230 ; local self-government, 52, 61, 89, 110–2, 230 ; wasteful user of land, 72–3 ; trading sites in reserves, 78 ; hut-tax, 82–3, 86 ; customs duties, 87–8 ; road rates, 91 ; existing laws and administrative systems, 99–103 ; definition of " Native," 122 ; legal status of natives, 125, 229–30 ; operation of native law, 129 ; marriage law, 130–3 ; law of succession, 133–4 ; missions in, 138–42 ; native education, *see* Education ; native churches, 192–207, 208

Cape, Native Locations Acts, 53–7, 78, 79

Cape Town, payment of labourers, 37 ; domestic service, 38 ; locations at, 40, 57

Casalis, M., 155, 160

Census, of population, 7, 98 ; of occupations, 9

Chiefs, position and jurisdiction of, 103, 104, 105, 106, 108–10, 113, 115, 116, 117–8

Chinese labour, 6 *n.*, 24, 25

Christian Express on Ethiopian Movement, 192 *n.*

Church of England, schools, in Cape

law of succession, 133 ; native education, *see* Education ; native churches, 193, 197, 199, 200, 206–9

Transvaal Labour Commission, 24, 42–4

Transvaal Mining Industry Commission, 45–6

Trappist, schools, 153 ; missionaries, 215

Treatment of labourers. *See* Labourers

Tribal system breaking down, 4, 5–6, 115–20, 227–9

Tsewu, Rev. E., 207

Tsomo district, individual tenure, 58

Turner, Bishop, African Methodist Episcopalian Church, 194, 195, 199

Uhlanga Church, 209

United Free Church, schools, 140, 146, 149 ; secessions from, 205-7, 209

Vanderkemp, Dr., 139

Van Lier, Dr., 138

Village Settlements, 65, 119, 204

Vryburg, Institution London Missionary Society near, 146, 176

Wages of natives, 12, 13, 23, 25, 26, 29, 30, 32, 34, 35, 36, 37, 38, 39, 46, 49

Warner, C. J., on individual tenure, 59, 60

Watersmeet, proposed institution at, 154

Weir, J. W., Inter-State Native College, 183

Wesleyan Methodist Missionary Society and education, 141, 142, 146 ; schools in Natal, 149, 153 ; in the Transvaal, 168, 170 ; in Orange River Colony, 171, 172 ; in Rhodesia, 173, 174 ; secessions from, 193, 194, 209 ; Wesleyan Church organisation, 222

White, Bishop, of Anglican Church, 200

Whiteside, Rev. J., *History of Wesleyan Methodist Church of South Africa*, 136 n.

Wilder, Rev. J. A., D.D., 209

Willoughby, Rev. H. W., 176

Witwatersrand, the, natives on, 21–33 ; Chinese labour, 24, 25

Witwatersrand, the, Native Labour Association, 28–33

Witzies Hoek, reserve at, 68–9

Women, their work, 1, 2 ; as domestic servants, 38, 49

Woodrooffe, Canon H. R., on land tenure, 61

Woollen goods sold to natives, 11, 87, 88

Zonnebloem College, 140, 145, 147, 148, 164

Zulu Congregational Church, 208–209

Zululand (*see also* Natal), area and population of, 7, 98 ; occupations of natives, 8–11 ; land tenure, 62–6 ; Land Commission, 64–5 ; hut- and poll-tax, 83, 92–6, 228 ; dog-tax, 88, 93 ; fees on passes, etc., 88 ; code of native laws, 103 ; diocese of, 140 ; education in, *see* Education ; American Mission, 149 ; Zulu Congregational Church, 208